Klairi Lykiardopoulou

THE MASTER

First Concepts - First Experiences

Volume 1

MEGAS SEIRIOS
Publications

ISBN: 978-960-7350-27-5

This book is published by **Megas Seirios Publications**, founded by the **Servers' Society Spiritual Centre** based in Athens, Greece. To find more information about the mission, works and activities of the Society and/or to place an order, please visit our website:
www.megas-seirios.gr

or contact us at:
9, Sarantaporou Street, Athens, Greece, P.O.: 111 44
e-mail: info@megas-seirios.gr
Tel.: +30 210 20 15 194
Fax: +30 210 22 30 864

Translation from Greek: Geoffrey Cox

Cover and book design: Marianna Smyrniotou

This book is dedicated to Master Dimitris Kakalidis and his wife, who – with their unwavering support – help the disciples of the Servers' Society on their path from human bonds to inner spiritual freedom.

ଓ

CONTENTS

FOREWORD

Mankind, life, people! Pain and relief, joy and unhappiness. Innumerable experiences, unanswered questions, but also many others to which an answer has come. These things, and many more, have been trying for four years now to find a way of expressing themselves on paper. I have written, and I have torn up what I have written. I have written again, and again I have torn it up. Then I stopped for a few months, waiting for new inspiration. How was I to impose some order on everything I wanted to say?

Then there came a telephone call from a stranger, who asked me: "Mrs Lykiardopoulou, what happened to that book about the Master which you said you were writing when 'Spiritual Healing' was published?" What could I say? "It's being written", I said. And it was true, because however much I tore up the manuscripts, the book was constantly being written in my mind. It wouldn't leave me alone, even when I wanted to forget it.

Nevertheless, one day my thoughts cleared, as though I'd realised why there was always something missing from my texts: because I was merely giving the findings of a task, an apprenticeship in life. But I wasn't describing its progress. And so I was leaving the most interesting feature out of the book, because it is these processes which are of greater importance – the difficulties, the failures, and the successes – until some result is produced.

Putting out of my mind any previous attempt, I began again from the beginning, this time in a new way. It was as if the book wrote itself, easily and quickly, because now the content sprang up freely from within me. This book is my very self, it is a part of what I have learnt, experienced, and understood in the last ten years of my life. It is the whole truth as I remember it, and as it is written down in the many files resulting from my learning experience.

The events which I recount do not always follow the chronological order in which they occurred. This is because an issue which concerns this discipleship is not rounded off within a short period of time, but makes frequent re-

appearances, until the knowledge is acquired and the corresponding translation into reality occurs. I have tried, of course, to draw the experiences which I describe from the first year of my discipleship, with a few exceptions, when it was necessary to include happenings from subsequent years.

The learning experience of each individual is a composite one. It is taken in by breathing, by eating, by making love. Sometimes the teachings are understood and sometimes not. If, however, you find yourself in the presence of a Master, of someone who helps you to understand what you are being taught, then your learning becomes conscious, life takes on another meaning. In my case, my footsteps led to the presence of a Master ten years ago. With his support, I began at that time to become a conscious pupil in the study of life and of myself, in order to find the truth, the meaning of existence.

What is to be found in the chapters that follow is just this – true experiences and real events as I lived them with the Master, who was the founder of the Servers' Society Spiritual Centre and delivered a teaching on self-knowledge, and a philosophical theory together with its practical application. With his help, the concept of the 'Master' expanded within me beyond a specific person, and I saw that we are all taught by everything every moment of our life.

It is about this Master that I speak in my book, about the Master-life, the Master-people, the Master-ourselves. And I demonstrate, through everything that I describe, how much that specific person, the Master of the Society, helped me to an understanding of the broad and deep concept of a 'Master'.

Precisely because the range of this concept is boundless, it cannot be covered in a single book. So I begin my account of it from the first basic concepts, and move on in the books which follow to more complex and more profound analyses. But corresponding to all the issues which I discuss, the experience, the realisation of the teaching in practice will always be given also. Because I believe that it is only in this way that a philosophy takes on its true value, when it is confirmed in life, in our selves, and when it becomes an experience and an awareness. Then it is that the Master finds conscious expression through mankind.

"Look deep within your mind.
It is there that truth is to be found,
there is the answer to your every question.
Look and you will find it."

Dimitris Kakalidis

Master Dimitris Kakalidis

☙

WHO IS THE MASTER?

From the very first moment that I met the Master, I felt the greatest ease in discussing with him any issue which was on my mind. The way in which he treated people made me feel certain that he would accept any misgiving on my part with simplicity, even if it was tedious, childish, or even irrational. Thus the dialectic between us developed quickly, without any pretexts on my part. We simply discussed my problems and my thinking about them together, without any obstacle.

I did, however, have one question which at that time I didn't dare to put into words. Ten years have passed, and I still remember my reactions over this matter. I wanted to ask my burning question, but I didn't do so. Because it didn't have to do with me and my own affairs, but, on the contrary, directly concerned him. And so I hesitated to say what I was thinking, and we had known one another for at least a year before I dared to ask my question.

The question with which I was so concerned at that time was about the way in which the Master began the conversation and the analyses. As he embarked on explaining some matter, he would say to the people he was speaking to: "The Master says – ", and then go on with the analysis. This sentence, I have to admit, produced various reactions in me – reactions which were not very favourable about the Master as a person. I wanted to interrupt him in the middle and say to him: "Who is this Master who says it? Isn't it you, my friend? If it's you, then why are you speaking in the third person? But if it's somebody else, why don't you tell us his name and set our minds at rest?"

These were the thoughts which never came to my lips; I considered them unacceptable and entirely inappropriate to my age. I was not spontaneous like the young people who were with the Master at that time, and I considered it unthinkable to offend – as I thought it would – someone with such a provocative question.

And so it remained without an answer, since it was not expressed in order to ask for my problem to be solved. There were times, I remember, when I was almost drowning in my own curiosity. And if, moreover, for personal reasons, I objected to the things the Master said, I was even more hostile to this third person who was supposed to be giving us the teaching. I reflected that whoever this unknown person was, he didn't know what he was talking about. His words went beyond the limits of reason, and the things he said about the potentialities of man or about life in general were certainly groundless. That's the way I felt one day, I remember, when the Master said that life is a game. But then I did burst out against this view, and I said to him: "What sort of game is this you're talking about now? The world is going to ruin, people are suffering; in order to achieve anything, you have to endure years of torment, and you call this a game? Come on now, I can't accept that." He didn't insist any further, as he saw that I was unable to understand what he meant, and I calmed down somewhat. But at other times, such calmness didn't come to me, and I was opposed to this seen or unseen Master who went on talking, and talking, and talking.

Although I hadn't put the controversial question, the Master began on his own to answer it, and this he continued to do always as the years went by. Thus, the first answer which I heard was that the Master is conscience and knowledge. I liked this, and began to search within myself for the voice of conscience, which would guide me to what was good and right. But the Master suddenly said that ignorance and error and imperfection are likewise a Master. I didn't like this, of course, because it is difficult to accept that wrong action can also lead to knowledge. But still I continued to work systematically in order to grasp these two opposing aspects of the Master's expression.

As I was taking the first unexplored steps within myself, I was given a new direction, which again disturbed me. The Master said that everything teaches us, all things are our fathers and teachers. In this sense, everything is our Master: a human being, or even an inanimate object can teach us something. Because I wanted to follow the Master's instructions, I began to study the forms in my surroundings, from the smallest to the biggest. Little by little, as this study continued, I discovered the truth of this teaching. I remember, many years later, when a new member of the Society also asked what 'the Master' meant, he replied: "Why, anything at all; don't personify the Master as one person, and don't become attached to him, because in that way you won't make progress. Look: I hit my hand against the wall and it hurts. Who is my Master? The wall is, because it teaches me not to strike my hand against hard objects. It's so simple!" I don't know, of course, whether this live performance conveyed the message and whether it could be understood that everything is our Master and Teacher. In my case it took time for me to accept this broad range of the meaning of the concept of the 'Master'.

While I was working to discover – I am talking still about the early days – the Master in all things, we were suddenly given a lesson about ancient Greece. I can remember the Master's words well enough, and I will attempt to relay them. He told us:

"In antiquity, the concept of the Master – Didaskalos – had great importance and inner value. Artists, writers, philosophers, and schoolteachers were addressed as 'masters'. In our own times, there is an unconscious trend towards avoiding this form of address. Masters have become professors, or 'sirs', or even friends whom the children call by their first names. This conceals a negative need, an avoidance of the inner Master who is so necessary for us. If I accept the form of address of 'Master', I do it so that this word will begin to be heard in Greece. What we lack is the profound concept of 'Master', and this must be revitalised for the good not only of Greece, but of the whole world. There are countries where experts are addressed as Masters, and this is very positive."

I was naturally very ready to embrace this analysis, but it conflicted with the previous interpretations, and I began to worry about this. So in the end what was I to do? To think of the Master as personified, or impersonal?

'Both' was the answer which was generated within me through experience and meditation as the years passed, that is, by going deeper into the matter in thought. Because the Master is all things: what is expressed consciously by a person, but also what passes unconsciously into us. I realised that the Master is the whole of life, the universe and the particle, the good and the bad, the visible and the invisible. It is all beings and non-beings, overall unity, universality, God. The Master says that the sole Master of all things is the higher Self, the Super Ego, that which is everywhere present and fills all things – the Supreme One God.

The ever-expanding concept of the Master, which touches on the Absolute, is perhaps the greatest problem which man has. How is he to understand, or even approach, the Absolute? And even if he is disposed to work towards this, what place should be taken in his consciousness by a Master in the form of a man, with imperfections and biological needs? Is it remotely possible that these have some connection with the Absolute, when they seem to be so distant from it? The Master himself answered these questions many times: "Do not make a god out of the Master", he told us. "All that he can do is to point the way, to broaden the consciousness, to speak about the Entity. All other ideas of human beings about Masters are their own projections; they are not the truth. Consciousness in man is a Master, but until this is revealed to him, he needs guidance, and this is what the Master gives."

The years passed and I steadily followed the discipleship for the revelation of the Truth. The veils of ignorance around me sometimes fell easily, sometimes with difficulty. The Master by his presence followed, as he always follows, the steps of all of us. He never changes; he remains the same, unmoving in the position which he has taken up. We, however, constantly change our stance towards him. We colour his words, his behaviour, and his actions in the light of our deficiencies. Sometimes we like him and sometimes we don't. There are times when we seek his teaching, and others when we avoid it, because we suspect that it will produce in us new causes for concern, which are often wearisome. However, whatever happens, I can now answer that original question: why it is that the Master speaks so often in the third person. The answer has come after many years of observation of this specific individual, and of other Masters whom I've happened to meet during this period. Deeper immersion in this issue, repeated meditation on the entity of the 'Master' have solved the problem for me.

A Master is not one who regards himself as some special person, with specialised knowledge and supernatural powers. He is, on the contrary, a person who has recognised in his individual existence the one and sole nature of all beings, the true entity. United in his consciousness with the one nature, all that he does is to speak of unity, to teach homogeneity, to urge his disciples to undertake that intellectual development which leads to the Absolute. It is precisely this that the use of the third person connotes: that he does not regard his words as his own, but that they are those of the entity, the one consciousness which also manifests itself through him. In any event, he sees the same thing in everybody and everything, the one boundless self with many facets.

Firmly grounded in a position of union, the Master teaches his disciples two things in parallel: the path of their individual evolution, and the externalisation of this evolution, so that the teaching will spread to more individuals. Thus, from the very early days, while I was learning to know myself, I was also learning at the same time how to perform a task for others. In the course of the years, this task took on very specific forms of expression in the Society. It was not confined simply to what each disciple did for his or her immediate environment, but working groups were also set up which performed services in various spheres. The first of these was the group which was concerned with theatre and puppet theatre. The younger people at that time organised performances and visited various institutions for children, to provide them with a few hours of recreation, all, of course, entirely selflessly.

By degrees, many sections performing services developed. One of these was, and continues to be up to the present, spiritual healing. This section consists of members who have an aptitude for becoming healers and work systematically for patients who seek help; naturally, they receive special teaching on the practice of spiritual healing. It was through this section that the need arose for there to be regular blood-donors for the patients, so that we set up a Blood Bank, which works in co-operation with the Laïko Hospital.

There have been periods when we have been very much concerned with giving support to drug addicts, providing them with special relaxation exercises, and monitoring their treatment closely. At other times we have provided financial support for indigent people who are unable to work. The stance of service which the Master teaches us is always to respond to whatever need presents itself, both in the psychological and spiritual as well as in the material field.

As the older disciples acquired the basic knowledge, the writing of lessons began, and later I myself began writing the first books on the teaching. Newer members are also trained in the written word, so that they can support the work of the publishing house which we have set up, with the constant purpose, of course, of disseminating spirituality.

In parallel with all this, the older disciples take on groups of young members, to whom they hand on the teaching, instruct in relaxation, and provide with forms of meditation. And, naturally, they are prepared for the founding of other societies where the task of responding to the burning needs of our age will be able to find other means of expression, depending upon the particular gifts of each disciple.

I have spoken in the first chapter of the book about the work of the Society – in very summary form, of course – because I think that in this way the concept of the 'Master' is complemented. A Master is the consciousness of man, which, as it is broadened with the help of Masters, leads the disciples at the same time to broaden their way of life and action; to concern themselves with others as they concern themselves with their own selves, by means of the insight that others and their self are one, they are the broader ontological self. By the service which he performs for his fellow human beings, the disciple firmly establishes the teaching and advances to essential union with the Master-consciousness within himself, in order to give him expression in practice and in his life with ever-increasing dynamism.

QUESTION AND ANSWER

I remember that day very well – even though it is now nearly 50 years ago. I happened to be all on my own at home, which was strange enough in itself, because my parents took care that their 11-year-old daughter should always have company. To begin with, I enjoyed my independence, I danced, I played, I sang. But time passed and I began to weary of the solitariness. In order to drive away my boredom, I opened the window and set about gazing at what was happening in the street.

For a few minutes I was deeply absorbed by the spectacle. I looked at the people, I made fun of their walk or their clothes, I felt sorry for some old people, I envied the young children who had friends with them. But without my realising what was happening, little by little this picture of the world began to blur, as though it had been transformed into an indefinite movement, an insubstantial coming and going of some blurred, distant figures. My head drooped on to the window sill, and I looked – without seeing it clearly – at the wall beneath it.

Then, entirely of its own accord, my hand started to score something on the wall with a hard object which I was absentmindedly holding. I was writing without thinking, but as soon as I had finished, I sat up, startled, as if I'd just returned from some long journey. With astonished eyes I read what had been written by my hand on the faded pink wall. There were two brief sentences, which read: "What is the world? What is life?"

I turned abruptly towards the room, to see if perhaps my mother had come back. Fortunately, I was still on my own. I didn't want anyone to see what I'd written on the wall, I had no confidence in how others would react when faced with my unexpected questionings.

The words were written upside down, they looked upwards, as if expecting to be read by the sky... As if they were looking to it for an answer. But from whom? From what you cannot grasp?

I closed the window and looked at the clock. In a little while the others would return, and this strange moment would be submerged in family life. The questionings had come to light, but I didn't dare at that time to address them to anyone. I was afraid, not only of their rejection, but above all of my disillusionment with the answers which I would be given. And so I chose to remain silent, and the only thing I did from time to time was to lean over the sill and read my own words in secret. Until, one day, the facade of the apartment block was redecorated, and the questions were hidden under the paint.

What was it, then, which at such an early age made me wonder about the meaning of life? What power brought my hand to the wall and guided it to write? What really is it which prompts a child to ask: "Mummy, is God dying?", and for her to answer: "What on earth are you talking about, child? You'd better not let your grandmother hear you, or you'll be for it!" What is the impulse which is poured out through a human being and makes him or her cry out in the face of injustice? "Why, oh why have I been treated so unfairly? How can people be like this?" How does the question arise, any questioning, and where does it spring from?

Who is to give the answer? Is it possible for man with his endless questions ever to be satisfied? We hasten to search. We rush as adolescents to find out, to live life. Because the answers reveal themselves only in rare cases, and if they come, it isn't always easy for us to understand them. And so the hunt begins, the unceasing need to acquire experiences. And when the body matures, the run becomes a walk, a slightly more stable course, but also a more weary one. Until our feet begin to seek for rest, as accumulated experiences impose a burden on them, sometimes an intolerable one.

Life cycles, cycles of quests, cycles of ignorance and knowledge. We all go through the same things; that's the way the world is made – or, I would rather say, that's the way we've made it ourselves. Birth and exultation, adolescence and love, growing older and responsibilities, and then old age with our thoughts turned towards death the unknown. Why, my God, all this? Where are we going and what are we doing?

The questions sprang from my lips in a torrent when I met the Master. If someone had asked me at that time what made me have confidence and believe that I would receive the right answers, I would have said that I didn't know. It is true that I didn't know why it was that with the Master the questions which for years had roosted within me were uncovered. Yes, it is a fact that on other occasions I had voiced them, but I had quickly sealed my lips again because I was never given the answer I was looking for. People, often more intelligent and better educated than myself, gave me some isolated items of knowledge, and I didn't know what to do with these. I classified them as well as I could, they opened up for me a little window of light, and then, among the host of unanswered questionings, the light was lost again.

With the Master things are different. He always gives the right answers, even though he himself maintains that he is not all-knowing. Often he listens like a child to the knowledge which others convey to him, or he refers us to various books for specific information. However, in spite of his gaps, the Master knows how to answer, as if he has concluded his studies in the school of life.

At the time when I met him, I was not concerned to discover what was the source of his knowledge of what he told us. All that concerned me was that I should receive the answers I wanted. I remember that when I first met him, I said to him: "And how do I know that what you have told me is right? You may not be what you appear, you may be the exact opposite, you may be an evil person, cunning and deceitful. So why should I believe you?" I thought that by this question I would embarrass him and that he wouldn't have anything to say to me. But his reply dumbfounded me and I never again was naive enough to repeat the same objection. He told me with great seriousness:

"No, you don't know whether what I've said is right, nor do you know what sort of a person I am. But you have your own self, and it knows. Search within yourself to find the truth, and if what we have said is confirmed for you, only then accept it." I said nothing; in any case, what could I have said? I returned home so full of new ideas that I needed two or three days to put them into some sort of order. And this happened every time that I received a new piece of teaching, at least in the early years of my discipleship. Understanding, assimilation, and acceptance of the concepts came little by little and often with many checks and objections. Much later, I acquired the necessary prerequisites for me to accept immediately what I was taught.

Naturally enough, as time passed, I saw something very simple. I saw that questions are generated in the mind and that it is there that they spring from. I also saw that it is within the same mind that the answers lie. If, however, a Master has the answers to the endless questions of his disciples, is he perhaps not a man? These are crazy ideas, of course, but they show the impasse encountered by someone who sees for the first time a different intellectual stance and function in his or her life. Because this thought tormented me considerably, the Master, who had realised from my attitude that I had it, asked me one day, completely out of the blue:

"What would you say, is the Master a man?"

Although his manner seemed a little mocking, I was not daunted and I answered hastily: "No!"

He looked at me then with seriousness and said:

"He's not a man? And what is this body? And the biological needs, what are they? If I'm not a man, what am I?"

I began to get confused and to realise that I had made a myth out of the concept of 'Master', precisely because I was unable to explain his way of thinking, his intellectual position. In order to help me, he gave me the answer himself:

"Of course I'm a man, how could I be anything else? And a very simple man at that, born of an ordinary family. Only I have a different intellectual attitude. That's all."

Often after that his words have come to my mind and have made me accept the Master in every human being, in conversations, in the mind, everywhere, and, above all, within myself. As I learnt to meditate with ever increasing substance, I often chose to address my questions to myself and from myself to derive the answers. I liked enormously to submerge myself in my being, to relax profoundly, and to open my mind to whatever came to me as an idea. It was as if everything wanted to meet my questionings, to reveal to me the unknown which is buried deep inside us. And so great is the power and the certainty which is drawn from our own self that without seeking this, you begin to be – with much hard work, of course, and over the years – an increasingly autonomous individual.

Question and answer within ourselves! Lack and supply within ourselves! Conception of an idea and bringing it to birth again within ourselves! If I had known when I was 11 years old where to find the one who knows, my own self, who would have given me the answers I was seeking, I would have become a totally different adult. I have frequently asked myself why I didn't know the Master even then. That, of course, would have been totally impossible, because biologically I am 12 years older than he is. But over and above that insuperable obstacle, I could have known some other Master, or even someone who had mastered something of what I did not have. But it didn't happen. And now I believe that this delay was no accident, because a momentary illumination does not mean that there is the necessary maturity for you to advance. It is simply one of those many unforeseen stimuli to the consciousness which come to reveal to you that beyond everything you see and know and experience, there are many other, unknown, factors, which you can search after and find.

In reading on the subject of children and of education generally, which is something which concerns me particularly as an educator, I saw somewhere a study about the schools of the future. In this there was a kind of envisioning about the direction which education should take. Among the many facts which were cited, what struck me most was the issue of meditation. It was suggested that children, from primary school age, should begin to learn relaxation and some simple patterns of meditation.

If we look at this idea in relation to the autonomy which every human being seeks to gain, it will be apparent how right it is. Because autonomy is simply the self-sufficiency, the completeness which comes when we arrive at the point of recognising that we are our own Master. Such an attainment is not arrived at, however, if it is not preceded by the quest for the inner Master, which can only be undertaken by meditation. All other mental conceptions are preparations for meditation, processes which precede a deeper and more substantive function. Just as a mother guides her child in its first steps of caring for itself physically, so the school should guide it towards becoming inwardly autonomous. If in the future educators have the appropriate training so that they themselves can work consciously for their own inner development, then the younger generations will progress more easily towards the solution of the various problems of humanity, which are due to immaturity of the consciousness.

In speaking of the subject of children and of education generally with the Master, I began to realise how much we are all children in certain things: tiring and demanding children who look to receive everything from other people and from life, or even from themselves – everything they need. And the Master has this to say on this subject:

"Man is a child and always will be, because this is his nature. But he is not only a child, he is mature and a wise elder, an entire integrated human being. The question is who will seek within themselves that maturity which will handle their childishness with confidence. Only the person who wishes also to find the other aspect of his nature will become the Master of the disciple who wishes to learn, his own immature self, that is. Maturity and immaturity exist together, question and answer are likewise within us, we ourselves are both. Let us not forget the teaching which we have received down the ages: 'Search within yourself to find the truth'. What else was it that Socrates taught when he spoke of the *daimonion* within himself? It was precisely this, the existence of knowledge within ignorance."

THE EGO AND OTHERS

I had been so enchanted by my submersion into myself in the early months of my discipleship that suddenly the idea of isolation began to flood into me. Oh, if only I could leave this noisy world! If only I could go up some mountain, to a monastic house, where you have all the time you want to be occupied with yourself and your problems! Because, really, what are you to do about the issues which so much concern you when you are constantly interrupted by phone calls, visitors, children, and a spouse? And all the same things over again, food, the house, tidying up... What meaning do all these things have when a new world has opened up within you?

Of course, these thoughts took me by surprise, and I stayed the same. I? Become a nun? When I had never been able to understand up till then why there were such people as monks. I? Leave behind the things of this world, when up to that time my chief concern had been that my family should function correctly? And yet these strange things happened to me, as if suddenly communion with others had become without interest for me, and sometimes intolerable.

Very cautiously I ventured one day to tell my thoughts to the Master. His reply upset me enormously. He told me that my idea concealed a tendency towards flight, a denial of reality, and a rejection of the service which it calls upon all of us to render to our families and to those around us generally. He added that I had adopted a self-centred position and a major objection to accepting the world as it is and working as well as I could in it and for it.

I left totally dejected by our meeting, and I even thought that the Master said things in the way which suited himself on each occasion. At other times I'd heard him talk about the importance of the work which can be done by evolved people when they live the monastic life. I didn't see at the time that it is one thing to decide consciously to withdraw from the things of this world in order to work in a different, inner, way for humanity, and quite another to shut yourself up in a monastery in order to get away from the human problems which are wearying you.

I was so disturbed – not, of course, because I wasn't going to put an idea into practice, one which was not, anyway, all that consciously formed, but mainly because I could see the wrong position that I had taken up – which resulted in something happening which had surprised me, because never before had such a thing occurred. I set out in my car to return home, and, as I have been driving for many years, I wasn't thinking at all about driving, which happened now automatically. However, that day nothing happened in a way which was familiar to me. I doubt whether I was travelling at as much as 20 kilometres an hour when I found myself up on the pavement, and a terrific noise was heard. The drive-shaft had broken, and I was looking at myself as if thunderstruck in the car, which had deviated from its course – and even from the most elementary rule of the road.

The episode was discussed with the Master, who analysed for me for the first time the meaning of the motor car. He said that it had to do with the body and its functioning. Man, as a spirit, finds himself within his body, which serves him for his life on the physical plane. It 'carries' him, that is, it helps him to live in the world, it is his bearer. The car is a similar field, since it again 'carries' man where he wants to go. He told me that the incident which had occurred showed that I was not harmonised with my body, and, accordingly, with the vehicle I was driving. And so I had lost control and caused a lot of damage to it, as is, in any event, the case with the body when it is not correctly supervised by the mind. I must point out here it was often proved after that with all the disciples that our inner state causes unexpected problems in the way in which we drive – and even in the vehicles themselves.

My next question, of course, when I had understood the Master's analysis, was what connection all this had with my desire to isolate myself from the world and from social life, since I had no problem with my body, as far as I knew. He replied that although I had no problem with my own body, I did have with that of others. I did not wish to remain among them, to care for their needs, to concern myself with the responsibilities of the physical plane. To put it briefly, I was rejecting anything that related to physical bearers and I was looking only for spiritual work – as I imagined it at that time – far removed from all earthly concerns. This, the Master added, showed a rejection of the physical world and is a mistaken attitude. Only if all forms are loved – bodies, material objects generally – can true calm and spirituality come.

In the whole of this conversation, another factor which made an impression on me revealed itself. I saw with perfect clarity that as long as the functioning of the human being concerns only the needs of the individual ego and is marked by indifference towards others, limitations continue, and any development is only apparent. Again, it was my own ego that I suddenly wanted to satisfy, but then, naturally, the Master, who speaks of love and union with everyone, didn't allow me to be trapped again in the same problem which has been perpetuated in humanity down the ages. He brought me to earth, a little abruptly, it is true, with regard to my responsibilities to others.

Who was now the Master in the whole of this happening? The man who patiently explained to me what had happened? Was it the car, which as if of its own accord climbed up on to the pavement, or was it myself, when I received a powerful message from my distress? Perhaps it doesn't matter if we find an answer to these questions, because what is important is that consciousness came via certain routes to teach me what I had to learn: that we are not separate, individual beings only, but that we are all going forward together, we exist together, we belong to a single whole. All the factors which were co-ordinated so that I could learn the necessary lesson were a Master, and, of course, it was the analysis given to me of the whole episode which contributed first and foremost to my understanding of it.

Perhaps the finding from this process will be considered very simple – that we all belong to a single whole. Is there anybody who doesn't know that? Again, the damage which was done so that a lesson could be learnt will be seen as excessive. But, as was demonstrated to me by countless episodes with many people who sought the guidance of the Master in the years that followed, both these ways on looking at it have something missing. Naturally, we all know that we are members of humanity, but how many people are there who experience, are aware of, and apply in practice such an obvious truth? I would say that very few do so constantly and that some do it only rarely. Most of us do not live as a whole, but as isolated individuals only. Our ego is not co-ordinated with other egos.

As to the matter of the car crash, I don't consider it as important as the lesson which I learnt from it. In any event, what goes on in the whole of our lives? Don't we collide with, don't we come into conflict with events, situations, our fellow-men? Isn't this our basic – perhaps our sole – problem every second? We say 'I and you', or 'them'. 'We' has not yet reached to the depths of its meaning; as to the 'one' which we all are, we are very far from making this a life experience.

We have one planet, and this we fragment into east and west. We are one humanity, and this is divided into factions, countries, peoples, rich and poor. A man and a woman seek to build a 'couple', and this comes into conflict with their separate egos. The Truth is one, but we turn it into doctrines and adapt it to the measure of our comprehension and our personal desires.

I have heard the need of the individual for separate, selfish satisfaction expressed so many times that it has ceased to make an impression on me. It is an unshakeable truth, but, as the Master says, it is only one aspect of the truth; there is always the other side of the coin. And this teaches us to see in man the truth about his great self, and not about his limited human ego. We are concerned so much with ourselves because we don't know; but, since we don't know, we must, quite simply, find out. And when we learn and understand, we will emerge from appearances and come to the essence. But how does such a change take place? Perhaps the answer to this question will not be very much liked, but I have found it to be the right one, at least this is how it has been confirmed for me. Knowledge comes through conflict, friction, problems, and difficulties. All these things come like pitiless, harsh teachers to overwhelm us, until at some point we ask ourselves: "Have I perhaps got something wrong?" If this question is asked, then a beginning has been made; everything else will take its course on its own. It is like piecing together a jigsaw puzzle. As its pieces go into their place, they are put together at an increasingly rapid rate, until the full picture is revealed.

This is how it is with the human ego – such a small piece of the jigsaw, which constantly cries out in order to validate itself. But on its own it can do nothing; whereas if it accepts its place in the whole, together with all the other egos, it will see what in reality it is.

I can remember a young man who constantly caused problems wherever he went. And then he would tell us: "My wife is to blame for the quarrels, my father is pig-headed, and that manager of ours behaves as though he knows everything". And so he found himself up against everything; it was as though an insuperable force was urging him to pit his body and his strength against everything. And if he was asked about his own behaviour, he would maintain that he was always right – it was only the others who were wrong.

The Master explained to him that all the others are certain aspects of himself, that he and his wife were a single thing. These words would usually infuriate him, he couldn't understand their meaning, because, there could be no doubt, he didn't wish to. If, even for a short while, he began to accept the concept of unity, he believed – or at least this is what his actions showed – he would lose his personality. In the end, he abandoned the teaching and continued to live as he had learnt to do since childhood.

Some of those who were disciples of the Master at that time expressed their sorrow, together with a tendency to be critical, about this young man's attitude. But the

Master said: “It doesn’t matter. Everybody is free to do what he wants. You should look at these things all in the same way. One person chooses one way of life, and someone else chooses a totally different one. No one has the right to interfere in man’s free will. Let each person choose his own road, because for him to do this means that this is necessary for him. It doesn’t matter if someone wants to stick to his familiar pattern of life, even if that limits him. At some point, perhaps even now as we are speaking, something new may come within him. ‘Judge not, that you be not judged’. Think only positively about everybody, and this is the greatest help which you can give them.”

THE MASTER IN DIFFUSION

One of the burning issues in my discussions with the Master was the issue of the 'Master in diffusion'. There were disciples much more receptive than I was to this concept, because I rebelled violently whenever I had to accept that there is also this manifestation of knowledge and consciousness, or, in other words, that knowledge is diffused everywhere, that it has no form, no body, and is literally invisible.

In general, the whole question of the formless, the non-material, the invisible seemed to me totally unreasonable and I wanted to reject it, to prove that the Master had got it wrong, and that what he told us was fantasy and wilful. I can remember his smile when he was faced with this resistance on my part, a smile which made me even more angry, because I felt like a young child with its father, who is amused by its childish tantrums. But as well as the smile, the analysis which he carried out for me, always with great patience, would also come.

Months passed, perhaps more than a year, before this concept began to penetrate my consciousness. During this time, there were battles with the Master, but also with myself. Every so often the truth would be demonstrated to me, and every so often I would reject it yet again. It is not all that easy to accept that the wisdom which, according to human reckoning, needs a human brain to develop and a human mouth to express itself can also be something else. And this something else, you are told, is without form, that is, it is nothing, or a state very close to nothing. How can nothing be wisdom? And even if we accept that it is, how is this proved to us?

At this point the Master would explain that formless wisdom takes on various forms in nature, in events, in happenings, in the innumerable symbols of the natural world. When we learn to see these and to analyse them, then wisdom is revealed to us. On this reasoning, we embarked upon a training in symbols, in order to be able to recognise the hidden meaning in them. Naturally, the Master used to say that we should not see each symbol in isolation, because then it gives us nothing more than a dry item of knowledge. We must always connect them with the happening of the moment, that is, with the specific event, conversation, or episode which is going on at that time.

Every sound, every colour, and every number is a symbol. Every object, or even a movement symbolises something. The posture of the body, the wind blowing, the rain falling – all conceal an inner idea. All these things and many other, innumerable features I should see as a manifestation of pansophia – 'all-wisdom' – the universal consciousness. And although I was enchanted by everything that I was learning, I fought against the idea of a formless consciousness which is projected in forms, and seems to be saying to us: "Wake up, you humans. Understand what I am teaching you, recognise me everywhere." I couldn't cope with such an expanse, it made me feel totally insignificant, a sub-particle of a sub-particle of some infinitesimal element in the universe.

And the specific lessons began – very specific lessons indeed. We were talking, for example, about the power of instinct, and at that moment the barking of a dog was heard – that is, the sound of an animal which operates through instinct. The Master was explaining to us the matter of sexual love, and suddenly a radio in the apartment block next door played the song which matched the analysis perfectly. We were discussing the significance of the number seven when we saw that the roses in the vase which somebody brought into the room at that moment were seven in number. "Coincidence", I would say. "Wisdom in nature", the Master would reply.

On the quiet, however, without admitting it even to myself, I began to make my own observations; because I somehow suspected that in the end the Master was right, that there is a world-wide consciousness which co-ordinates even the tiniest detail in the world, since the whole cosmos is in the last analysis one boundless unity. So many proofs of this were given to me every day that a whole book could be written about them.

At one time I was working on the issue of love, which was a matter of constant concern to me, as I was trying to see how love manifests itself in everyday life. I knew that all colours symbolise something, and that pink is the symbol of love.

I was out in the country one day with my little grandson, and while he was playing, my mind was circling round and round the same subject. Suddenly, and without anything leading up to this, the child pointed to a red apple which appeared on the print tablecloth, and said to me: "A little white is needed here". And then he carried on playing as if he hadn't said anything to me.

I was amazed. Because if we mix red with white, naturally, we get pink, that is, the symbol of love which I was turning over in my mind. But it wasn't only the projection of the symbol which took me by surprise; my grandson had shown me, totally involuntarily, of course, how love is born. He had said that to the red, which I had learnt means desire, white – purity – must be added. In other words, the lesson which I took from the lips of a child was that when desires are purified, then love comes.

But who made the child speak at that moment? Why was there a red apple on the tablecloth, and why suddenly did my grandson show a liking for the colour pink? And, finally, why did all this happen at a time when I was working on the issue of love? However much I wanted to reject the existence of a diffused consciousness which directs everything, it was impossible for me to do it, because events were demonstrating the opposite to me. The knowledge which I lacked at that period was there, somewhere in the unconscious. The question within me was very intense, and its power drew out, as if by magnetism, the appropriate answer. Because I couldn't find it on my own, the little boy acted as something like a conduit and projected it through symbols, without, of course, realising anything of this.

Another frequent occurrence which confirmed for me the existence of the Master in diffusion was the unexpected replies I received when I was meditating. Whenever I was negotiating an issue and couldn't sort it out and find a solution, this was given to me in some other way. One morning I was studying the meaning of life; I wanted to understand what it is in the last analysis, how it operates, what it does. As I couldn't find an answer which satisfied me, I continued to go round in the same mental circles, coming back to the same question: "What is life?" Suddenly a voice was heard in the street, the voice of a knife-sharpener who was shouting: "The wheel, the wheel, the wheel!" I was startled and astonished, and my mind was illuminated: "But of course, this is life, the wheel, the turning wheel, which sets everything in motion, and is moved by energies and powers!" The voice in the street faded way, and I, by the help of the concept of the wheel, continued to explore in depth the subject I was studying.

Another time, again, because I was having difficulties with someone I knew, I wanted to find out how I should handle the situation. I had tried many things, I had tried to put right our relationship with patience, with reasoning, with anger, with analysis – nothing worked. Was there anything, in the end, I hadn't done, anything I hadn't tried? My self didn't know, or didn't want to bring to light, a right answer. Then, although I was in deep meditation, the fluttering of a bird made me open my eyes. On the sill of the open window a pure white pigeon was sitting and looking at me. Then I understood! I had not given my pure power of soul and love to this person. Only this would overcome our difficulties – the giving of the power of the spirit, whose symbol is the dove. Quite involuntarily at that moment I felt for the first time a feeling of thankfulness spring from within me for the diffuse Master, who watches all things and helps them to evolve.

However, when someone is insistent and stubborn, as I was at that time, the truth is not accepted, however glaringly it presents itself before them. And such a person doesn't accept it, because there is something which he or she doesn't know, or fears. And what I was afraid of, as I have said, was the dimension of boundlessness: if I accepted this, I would – so I thought – become small and insignificant, and I thought I would be lost. I was at that period incapable of conceiving that if you accept the infinite and unite yourself with it, you are not lost, but, on the contrary, you pass into another state of consciousness, you grow up, you become one with everything, and you become diffuse yourself.

The Master, in order to liberate me from the problem, worked systematically with me in a variety of ways. One of these was arithmosophia – the wisdom of numbers – which he taught to all his disciples. Since I always needed to study concepts in depth, he urged me also to read the relevant books on the subject, and in these I found the inner meaning of every number – the idea which each number expresses. Thus I had acquired a considerable body of knowledge about them and could use them accordingly by making various combinations, additions, subtractions, and so on.

What puzzled me was why the Master supplied the other disciples only with a certain amount of information about numerology, but spent whole hours on the subject with me. Sometimes I found this tiring and I was in no mood for counting, for thinking in numbers and putting them together and analysing them. It seemed to me that all the teaching I was receiving – at that time, of course – was nothing more than a number. "What's happened to the other issues?" I wondered from time to time. But the Master kept on bringing up the same subject, as if it were of vital importance. Now, of course, I know why he did this. Because, quite simply, as my mind needed tangible proofs in order for me to accept the existence of the entity, the diffuse essence, and knowledge, very specific numbers were precisely what would demonstrate the truth to me.

I should point out here that, depending upon the individual nature of the disciple and the special processes which were taking place within him or her in each case, the Master uses differing learning patterns. And so in my case he worked with me at that time through numbers, so that I could understand what it was that I was unable or unwilling to see. As was proved by the result, he was absolutely right, and numbers gave me substantive help.

This intensive course of learning lasted for more than three months. I remember it very well because it was summer and we used to sit in the Society's little garden, which at the time had gravel under foot. As soon as I joined the Master, whatever subject of conversation I brought up, after, of course, he had first given his reply, he would then ask me for confirmation through numbers. If we were talking about knowledge, whose number is five, he would tell me to pluck, with my eyes closed, a twig from the tree so we could see whether in reality it had five leaves. If we talked about the Master, who is symbolised by nine, he would ask me to count the money in my purse, to see if its total gave the number nine. Confirmation came constantly, and yet, though I could see it with total clarity before me, I still had my reservations about diffuse wisdom.

All this was, of course, somewhat tiring. I had ended up counting legs, heads, chairs, glasses on the table, gravel in my fists, car numbers – anything. Even when I was apart from the Master I carried on with the counting, how many steps I was taking, how many times the telephone rang... And in every case I carried out the analyses which I had been taught and sought confirmation all the time.

As all this work was going on, I began to study and meditate on the matter. Even if I didn't do this on my own, the numbers would come without my wishing it, to provide some elements of assistance. Thus, one day when I was meditating on something – I can't remember exactly what – the number 121 came as an answer. As I wasn't sure about this, I asked the Master if 121 was right in relation to the general issue I was dealing with. "Certainly it is", he replied. "But let's look at this in greater detail". He picked up in his hand some small pebbles from the gravel and, when he had done some additions and subtractions, told me that they gave the right number. I didn't accept this confirmation. Although as far as he was concerned the answer had come, the Master made a second test with a fresh fistful of pebbles. Again sums, again confirmation for the Master, but again rejection in my part. The same thing happened five or six times, but I continued to deny the result.

Then what we call 'a Master's anger' occurred. This is not anger as we usually describe it, but a force which comes to break down mistaken notions and forms of resistance. His powerful voice startled me: "What on earth is it that you want in order to believe? Do you want me to pick up precisely 121 pebbles? Will that convince you? If you are going to believe that way, then so be it." I looked at him with very mixed feelings; although I had been shattered by his voice, at the same time I felt very sarcastic about his belief that it was remotely possible that he could pick up in his fist exactly 121 pebbles. And I waited, ready to deride him for such a naive thought.

Calmly, the Master put his hand into the pebbles; he moved it about a little in order to gather them up, closed his fist, and lifted it up. Then he rested it on the table, opened it, and the pebbles spread out. Anxiously I began to count: 'One, two, three ... 121!' Incredible! I was at a loss, I was thunderstruck, I couldn't believe my eyes. Come on, it wasn't possible. Had I perhaps made a mistake? I counted again from the beginning. Again 121. That was the end of the matter. Wisdom in nature had overcome me. It had proved much greater than myself.

Here the problem ended. The existence of the Master in diffusion had now been confirmed unshakeably. The Master said nothing; the truth spoke for itself. He had proved it by his faith and his patience. Nor did I speak, but inside myself I thanked him, because suddenly I felt a great calm. The idea of world consciousness which is within everything was a beginning for me, a beginning of security and serenity. The lesson in numerology was at an end, since it had fulfilled its purpose. New paths were opened up in my discipleship. Some of these were easy and some were difficult, to some there was resistance and to others there wasn't. But whatever we disciples did, the Master remained firm in his position, and showed us the way which leads to the Entity, to God.

THE TEACHING OF SYNTHESIS

When I first went to the Society, I met there some young people who had begun their discipleship a few months earlier. From these I learnt various things about the lessons and the teaching they were receiving. Among other things, they informed me that the teaching was a 'synthesis' – it was 'composite'. I must admit that this explanation told me nothing. I had no idea what 'synthesis' could mean in a course of learning, nor, in any event, was I particularly concerned to find out. The only thing I wanted at that time was to find a way of life which was more dynamic and calmer than that which I had lived up to then.

The strange thing with me was that up to the time when I met the Master I had not concerned myself at all with such spiritual matters. Although I had been an avid reader since childhood, texts dealing with esoteric, spiritual, or occult matters had never come into my hands. Nor had I met anyone likely to suggest anything of the sort, such as work at a spiritual centre, to me. And it made an impression on me later when I saw that many of the members who came to the Society had had quite a number of advanced experiences and had studied various matters with an affinity with the teaching.

This total ignorance meant that I was indifferent when faced with the title 'Synthesis', when the only thing which I wanted was self-knowledge and autonomy. But my indifference didn't last long. Soon my interest was stirred and I began to investigate what 'synthesis' meant. Because, as the primary needs were allayed, my curiosity spread to other matters, and naturally one of these was the meaning of 'composite' teaching, which, in any event, concerned me directly. Thus, I wanted to know what exactly I was being taught, and how I received the lessons.

A first conception was that the Master accepted all philosophical, religious, etc. trends, and through a synthesis of them spoke to us of the one Entity, which is all things, and is in all things, without divisions. Through this approach any dogmatic positions, prejudices, or oppositions are broken down, since the reference for all things is God alone, the one and only field.

As a theory and an intellectual conception I was in complete agreement with this idea. I had always maintained that I was against racialism, dogmatism, and the separation of races. But in practice things were entirely different. It's one thing to believe that people must be united with one another and with the whole of life, and another to implement this idea and apply it in practice: not to prefer, that is, one job to another, to wish to have the company of a certain person, but not to avoid someone else. Here things become incredibly difficult. If, however, you don't start out from such simple everyday matters, how is it possible for you to advance to deeper and more substantive concepts?

And so the application of the teaching in practice began. Or rather, the fight, the conflict, the resistance and the constant quarrels began, chiefly with the Master, who every day brought us a new pattern, a new idea for us to express. Sometimes I wanted to shout out: "For heaven's sake! Aren't you going to leave anything alone? Are you going to demolish everything, are you going to alter everything all the time? Let us get used to something and settle down a bit."

There are innumerable examples. When I went to the Society, I found all the rooms freshly painted in soft shades. But before two or three months had passed, the

Master said that they would all have to be repainted in one neutral colour only, because this would change the field. What did this mean would change?

As he told us at the time, the change would help the disciples not to have a preference for any particular colour. And why shouldn't they have? Because when you prefer a colour and give yourself to it – and the same applies to all issues – you are not essentially free. The Master was routing the teaching on union via a bucket of paint! We tormented ourselves for two or three hours until we'd made the mixture of the colours, which resulted in a very soft biege. It often came into my mind during those days to get up and leave, or to give the bucket a kick for taking our time away from other things. Was this the sort of thing I'd come to learn at the Society? Wouldn't I be better off sitting at home?

This was one of the simpler – and, relatively, more painless – activities which went on at the Society. In any case, the painting didn't take long, it was soon over. But many other things were incredibly difficult and frequently annoyed me personally. I remember that once a girl complained that she had a pain in the stomach, and the Master told her: "Go and practise relaxation, and apply spiritual self-healing; you haven't anything wrong with you". A fine answer, I was delighted with it, it suited me completely. The idea of a therapy through meditation – this is what I wanted to do all the time. But when – a few days later – I told the Master that I had a headache, the answer was: "Take an aspirin, Mrs Klairi. Why are you telling me?" An aspirin! So I was not to practise meditation. Hadn't he taught us self-healing? Why was he altering his words now? I said nothing to him, but when I left him, I was in a state of irritation, wondering why he said some things to one person and something different to somebody else. It was as if he had stolen something from me – the pleasure of meditation. How was I to understand at that time that the reason why he did that was that I had arrived at the point where all I wanted to do was to meditate from morn till night. And, of course, this attachment, like any other attachment, is an obstacle to learning, even if through meditation you can make substantive progress; because the most essential thing of all is to be free.

Naturally, the concepts of 'attachment' and 'freedom' were not clear in my mind, and for that reason I didn't understand the way the Master worked. There was a room at the Society which, if it had had a tongue to speak, would have voiced the most dreadful complaints, because every so often we would weary it with alterations. We would nail shelves to the wall and turn it into a reading-room, we would take down the shelves and convert it into a room for convivial gatherings, the gatherings would stop, and we would fill it with chairs, so that group lessons could be held there. But even the chairs didn't stay put; sometimes they were arranged in a circle, sometimes one behind the other, facing in a different direction each time. "Knit, and then unravel, so you have something to do." The life of the disciples was something like that at that period. And the Master had a finger in everything, even down to the tiniest detail.

Sometimes I saw him as a completely crazy craftsman who built a wall one day and the next day pulled it down in order to build another one. But in this way he didn't leave us a single minute in which to curl up in any 'nest'. I would have liked to say to him – if I had dared to do so: "OK. Tell me, are you a Master of synthesis, composition – or of antithesis, or even of decomposition?" But how was I to dare? Because however much I constantly raised objections over many issues, there were many others which I buried inside myself: something told me that I shouldn't go too far. Then, in spite of the – apparent – element of absurdity in what went on, I began to recognise that in the end these changes served a purpose. They gave us a new mood, new ideas, a different approach to things, and, above all, they broke down for us forms of dependence on external patterns.

Much later, when I had begun to make my discipleship conscious, I worked to understand what synthesis is and what it means to accept all currents. Over and above the recognition of the homogeneity of all theories of the cosmos, synthesis is also an everyday practice. It is, I would say, the merging, the union of opposing factors, which presupposes their dissolution. This occurs in nature, in the whole of the natural world, but it also happens in the consciousness, that is, in the merging of all ideas into one idea, which is the Entity. In order for a synthesis to take place, established situations must be disrupted and constantly regenerated in a new form. This is what the Master was doing with all his re-arrangements and reshapings.

With the passage of time, the changes passed from the physical field more to the spiritual. Although they did not cease entirely with regard to space or clothes or any day-to-day work, I would nevertheless say that changes of this kind diminished perceptibly and greater emphasis was placed on disciple's inner attitudes. If, for example, someone showed an aptitude for the study of special issues by means of the relevant books, the Master encouraged that aptitude. If, however, in the course of time an excess – and probably an avoidance of other kinds of work – became apparent, the advice given would be to cut down on reading and that the disciple should fill the gaps which this had left.

A few years before my discipleship began, I had begun to involve myself in an amateur way with painting. I spent many hours a day with my paints and my canvases, which provided me with a means of expression.

And so, later, when I was going to the Master, I took my paintings along with my problems. In the early months, we discussed every work which I had produced, each colour or pattern which I had painted. In addition, following his advice, I also read various texts on the technique of painting. I continued to paint, and I couldn't at that time imagine how it would ever be possible to abandon it.

For as long as I needed this particular form of release, I had the encouragement of the Master, in spite of the fact that I found him very strict in his judgments. When, as the months passed, I began to take up writing, meditation, and certain responsibilities in the Society, he gave me to understanding that painting was no longer necessary for me, that this cycle had at some point been completed. I now know that I had a certain dependence on my works: they were not the works of some creative force, but the result of certain emotional impasses.

The transition from painting to other activities took place by means of a number of processes, which I will not describe at present, because they have to do with other issues concerned with my discipleship. What I wish to make clear by this example is that whenever the inner positioning of a disciple is the product of weakness, as the need for painting at the time was for me, the Master breaks this down by whatever means. By giving me at that point a more dynamic job, he freed me from my attachment to painting. Later, when I again showed a desire to paint, he always advised me to do so, but to cultivate within myself a different stance – more dynamic and without forms of dependence.

One of these 'dissolutions', as we then called the changes brought about by the Master, happened in the second year of my discipleship. This wounded me a good deal, and I was unable to stand it for a considerable length of time. That year I had begun to convey the teaching I was receiving to the newer members of the Society. Some groups had been formed, and I had written the first lessons and so was able to provide an elementary outline, of which I had a good grasp.

Before these groups were formed, the Master gave me a veritable scorching with his words; he said it was wrong for me to have learnt so many things and not to hand them on to others. He urged me to express myself more, to open up to the people who came to the Society, not to remain inactive in this area. It took some time for me to overcome my doubts – about whether I knew enough, whether the others would accept me as their group leader – whether I would be able to manage it, in other words. The more I had doubts about myself, the more he pressed me to begin, telling me that everything would be fine.

In fact, the groups started, and with the help of the Master made progress. Moreover, I began to like my new role, so that I couldn't wait for the next meeting with the members, as I was beginning to form a bond with them. Whereas a short time before I'd avoided this responsibility, I soon began to need it, and it was necessary for me. But what Master allows his disciple to be dependent upon anything, even if that is the spreading of the teaching itself?

And so the inevitable occurred. One day the Master summoned me and told me that my relation with the groups must be dissolved, that I must hand them over to someone else, that I must cease entirely to be involved with them. He also carried out an analysis of my attitude, but I wasn't listening to him; what I had heard was enough for me. Nor did I raise any objection this time, I had no anger, just sorrow. I went down to the first floor and sat in the office like a lost soul. And what would I do now without the groups? What would be the point of my life? It is apparent from these thoughts, of course, that my stance was not a right one; it was not a stance of independence and simple service, since I was deriving self-centred satisfaction from the lessons I was giving.

The solution to the problem was given to me after a little while by the Master, because I was not calm enough to find it for myself. He told me that the time had come for me to speak on a person-to-person basis with people about their special problems in individual meetings. In this way a new pattern of contacts with members of the

Society would begin, and this in itself would help me to escape from dependence. The individual appointments did not occur on regular days, but only when someone needed such contact, and so no habit was formed. Then again, on most occasions the person who wished to discuss a matter of his or her own was in great need of help and this then taught me to forget my own needs in order to respond to those of others. Of course, there were moments when I still missed the groups, but with the passage of time this lack disappeared completely.

A new year was beginning, autumn, new members, new re-arrangements, new combinations. My work with the Society became more composite. While I continued the individual appointments, I began to work with the groups again. I saw how 'dissolution', which some months before had upset me so much, had essentially changed me. The experience of the personal contacts had begun to awake within me a stance of response, reducing correspondingly my need for satisfaction. It was not the Master's intention to destroy a pattern of functioning, but, on the contrary, to build it on stronger foundations, composing it together with another. The two patterns together gave me a more expanded mode of operation, but this was only a part of another, even broader. Because while I was handing on the knowledge which I had received, I continued to be taught by the Master. It was as if I were inhaling certain knowledge, and then exhaling it so that it could be taken by those who needed it. This, however, is a part only of a greater and more composite whole, since the knowledge which we all receive is given through everything – the Master in diffusion, the Master life. And we again teach something, consciously or unconsciously, to others, maybe by our mere presence, or even by our mistakes.

In studying the laws of the natural world, we see a similar function of synthesis of antitheses for the building of new wholes. Day and night give us the 24-hour period, and 365 of these make a year. And this year is only one of the innumerable circlings of the earth around the sun. But the sun is not eternal; as one theory goes, all the solar systems will one day break up.

Where is all this leading? To the final assimilation of the many into one, to the final synthesis of all things into the Unit. The teaching of synthesis, with all the dissolutions which it involves, and through the building up of small, infinitesimal, we could say, wholes, has as its sole purpose the union of man with the Entity. How many years it took me to accept that the mixing of the paints in a bucket, the nailing up and taking down of the shelves, the breaking up of the groups, and endless other activities had this purpose alone!

Mankind in its entirety is working for synthesis, even if it doesn't always do so consciously. What else is the building up of organisations, associations, and societies but an attempt at composite functioning? What else is the co-operation of states, of religions, of political parties but a synthesis? In the chaos which prevails on the planet and in spite of all the forms of resistance of individuals, new trends are making their appearance which prove man's desire to broaden himself by transcending his personal needs and stretching out his mind to new ideas and the corresponding actions.

The teaching of synthesis, which unites all the currents in a single current of life, is very broad and multifarious. Only an elementary account of it is given in the present text, in order to show my initial relation with it. In the texts which follow, I will revert to this issue, which is so vital, particularly at the present time, a time of great antitheses, changes, and amalgamations.

The Master, in speaking of the present time, says that it is the beginning of the New Age. He stresses that the changes which are taking place today on the planet are preparing the ground for the new souls, the coming generations. Even though we are going through difficult moments, these are necessary processes for the evolution of mankind, which has already developed a mind, so as to be able to use it for the evolution of the soul and the development of the spirit. The Master speaks of substantive changes in education, in the relations between man and woman, in the collaboration between states – in general, in the whole structure of society. Already people are speaking of the New Age, and the astrologers speak of the age of Aquarius, which began a few years ago, a period of synthesis, merging, and new ideas. The inner correspondence of all external events lies, as will be obvious, in the inner synthesis of the currents in the Unit. We are advancing towards the conquest of the pan-human consciousness, and the more this is attained, the more it will manifest itself through sympathy between groups and their collaboration in every sphere – political, governmental, economic, religious, among others.

"We are all learners together", the Master says, "through the difficulties of the present, so that we can build the better world of the future, the New Age".

LIFE IS OUR MASTER

I had had a dream, a very strange dream. And, moreover, I had it on the night before my first meeting with the Master, which had been arranged for the next day. I had been so struck by what I had dreamt that I sat down and wrote an account of it with all the details, providing some explanations of its meaning. My interest in the significance of dreams had started when I read in a book certain analyses of what they mean. From then on, I too began to seek an interpretation to my dreams, and when a dream made a special impression on me, I would write it down immediately, because I believed that it would reveal something to me if I studied it carefully.

In the dream I had that night, I was in my house, which appeared in two differing pictures. One of these was exactly as I knew it, only, although it was full of members of my family, it was at the same time completely empty. And so I went from room to room not knowing what to do and with the strange feeling that some important features were missing. The other picture of the house was like a circular diagram, which again I looked at without knowing what I was doing inside it. There was something missing from it, as if the points had been moved from their place, as if there were no central point, no centre.

Next to me was an older woman, a teacher. I discussed with her my problem: what I was to do in this strange house of mine with its two forms. I also discussed it with my little niece, who was her pupil and who at that time was on some trip with other children and was enjoying herself, having a very good time.

Suddenly, as I was looking at my house – the one that was like a diagram – I saw where the central point was. And the voice of the teacher was heard saying: "There's no need for you to do anything at the various points. Just push so that the wheel turns." Because the circular diagram had turned into a toothed wheel!

When I woke up, I wrote down my thoughts about what I had dreamt about. My first thought was: "So there's my job, I have to push the wheel of life of my family". But then I changed my mind and wrote: "What kind of a job is this, pushing a wheel? I would like to have some other role, the one my niece has". But in the end I changed my mind again and wrote: "How stupid I am! Is there a more important job than the movement of the wheel? Perhaps it's a little obscure, but without it, nothing is achieved."

These thoughts provide, of course, some particulars about the dream, but they don't cover it globally. Today, after the endless analyses and breaking down of symbols which I have been taught by the Master, I can see the deeper meaning of the dream. Of the two pictures of the house, the first shows its external appearance, that is, its areas with the members of the family, and the second the inner meaning of each family, which in essence is a circle, a wheel. It is a 'family circle', as many are accustomed to call it. Both in its external and in its inner form, a deficiency appeared in the dream, a breaking up of the individuals, because there was no dynamic centre to direct them properly.

The presence of the woman teacher next to me is a figure of the inner Master, of the consciousness, which in the dream was counselling me to take up the dynamic position of the centre, to undertake my responsibilities in full within the family.

There is, however, another presence – the little girl who was enjoying herself. This is the hidden quality of childhood, which wants to stay with a non-responsible function of games and visits.

In the dream, the three aspects of man are projected: the Master, the child, and the intermediate stage, the disciple, who is being trained by the Master, but vacillates in his decisions, because he is still very immature. When I went to the Master next day and, among other things, read my dream to him, he didn't at that time make many comments, which, in any case, would not have helped me, because I had had no preparation for deeper analyses. He simply told me to pay special attention to the concept of the wheel and its centre. I now see that what he had pointed out to me was that man must become dynamic and himself direct the energies and powers of life, remaining steady in the central position of the axis, which, in other words, I would say is the helm of life.

Here I must take the opportunity of saying that many people, a day or two before meeting a Master, have dreams of particular significance. Naturally, it should not be thought that this happens because of some mysterious intervention on the part of the Master, who may not even have been told of the forthcoming meeting. It happens only with the intervention of the inner Master. What happens is simple and by no means inexplicable, as it often seems to be. As the soul of man is searching for something, what he is looking for is projected by symbols in his dream, that is, it always relates to the state of the soul of the individual. And so, as I was looking for a Master and a teaching, the answer came in my sleep, before it had found expression on the natural plane. The same happens with other future disciples.

As to the dynamic position which I saw I should express, I couldn't at that time understand what this meant. Nor was I quick to understand it with the teaching I was receiving. The will was there within me, but the knowledge was missing; faith in the power of man, and the method, the specific functions, that is, which I had to put into practice were missing. My inability to realise this dynamic stance became apparent immediately after the first lessons with the Master.

At that time, like every new convert, I wanted to convey everything I was learning to whoever I came across. I didn't know that my attitude gave rise to opposition, particularly in those who had a different approach to what I was saying. Nor did I imagine, as I was an absolute beginner in my discipleship, that very often I was far from clear and consistent in my views.

As I was speaking one day to an acquaintance of mine, and when I had explained to him the issue of positive forces in man, I thought that he had fully understood and agreed with me. But it was exactly the opposite. For everything positive that I cited, he put forward its negative. And, moreover, he supported himself with historical facts, which I found difficult to refute. I got angry, raised my voice, but it was as if he couldn't hear me. I felt that he was making fun, just to irritate me, of all the concepts I had explained to him. In the end, as I looked at him in total disillusionment, he asked me what I thought about his extensive historical knowledge. Wasn't he good at it?

I didn't reply. I had been disillusioned as never before. When, later, such episodes were repeated with others, I resolved not to speak again. I didn't investigate at that time to see what possible mistakes I was making in the way in which I held these conversations or in the emotions I felt about my friends and acquaintances. Because suddenly it was as if I was on my own. But I didn't give up. I would go ahead and nothing would stop me now, in spite of the fact that I thought that I and the others were living in two different worlds.

Although I stopped handing on the teaching to those who didn't wish to hear it, my contacts with them nevertheless continued, with all the usual minor frictions, oppositions, and conflicts which human beings have. I had become particularly sensitive to everything, and my feelings seemed to absorb everything which others emitted. If someone was talkative, their talkativeness annoyed me in a way it had never done before. If they were sad, I suffered together with them. If they took no notice of me, I was completely shattered.

I discussed everything that I felt with the Master, who gave me certain simple instructions so that I could learn to live more harmoniously. One of these was that I should see in every person the positive, the right, the strong. I shouldn't think at all about his negative characteristics, because the more I thought of these, the more they would grow in my mind and would seem to me appalling, monstrous. I should multiply the positive characteristics by my thoughts, in the belief that these thoughts would also influence the other positively.

I began to put the Master's lesson into practice, though it seemed to me a little improbable that it would have any positive result. But in most cases – and this always puzzled me – the people changed when I turned a blind eye to their errors and imperfections. As if my positive thoughts passed into them and made them better and much calmer than usual. But this didn't always happen, and I turned tired of constantly thinking the same thoughts -that they were all good. Failure discouraged me, as if I had lost something which I had gained laboriously, as I believed. I saw with time and observation that life's biggest problem is relations between people.

I repeatedly brought up the issue with the Master, and when failure grew greater, I took in out on him. Since I couldn't bear to accept my own weaknesses, I said that he was to blame and that the instructions he had given me were a mistake. I didn't suspect that my own way of carrying out his advice was a mistake.

The usual conversation between us went as follows: "I can't understand, Master, what you are telling me. How is it possible for me to see a lazy, a jealous, an aggressive person as good?" "You are not doing it with all your will, that's why it's not working." "How can you say that?" I would answer back immediately. "I put every effort into making it happen". "Effort isn't needed, Mrs Klairi. Simply think the thought which you should and everything will happen of its own accord". When I heard this reply, I would lose control. "What do you mean, effort is not needed? Why do we say, then, 'effort is sufficient'? How can anything be done without effort?" Then the Master would explain: "You don't want to hear what I'm telling you. Just pay attention a moment. I think something positive, and the energy of my thought goes to the recipient. That changes him by itself and effort has no place."

The Master spoke and I listened, often I didn't listen properly, or I forgot what he had told me when I encountered some new difficulties. I entered into life attempting to become the centre of the wheel, the effort gave rise to tension, and the tension caused fatigue. I realised that from the time I started my discipleship, I had many more ups and downs than I had previously. I was sometimes up in heaven, and sometimes down in hell. Happiness and misery played a wicked game with me. I didn't understand why this was happening and it took me some time to find out.

What I discovered from experience was that the disciple, as his mind wants to grasp new concepts and as his body is energised through meditation, becomes more sensitive to all currents. Until he develops the necessary knowledge and the power within him is revealed – to some degree, of course – it is natural for him to be vulnerable. This doesn't last long, because life itself forces him to make use of the things – albeit a few – that he has learnt. And it is then that he handles situations more calmly, until at some point he becomes the centre of them, and does not fear others or himself. I was learning, then, with pain and anxiety that as long as the steady power was not coming from within me, the problem would continue.

Once when many difficult situations had built up, I decided that the discipleship was over for me; it wasn't doing anything for me. And I told the Master that I was leaving, I was giving it up, I was abandoning everything. He looked at me seriously, but I could detect a teasing smile in his manner: "And where will you go?" he asked me. "I'll go, it's finished. I can't stand this teaching any longer. It will drive me mad." A conversation followed about what I would do if I left, and perhaps it was better to re-think the whole issue, but as I was unshakeable in my decision, the Master said: "Very well. Go." And in fact I said my farewells and left as quietly as possible.

This decision lasted two days. On the third, I returned to the Society and never again gave up my discipleship. As I'd been left on my own, I saw that life is in any event difficult, which, in any case, I knew well from all my previous experiences. And since it was difficult, why not follow a path which had already been proved to me correct plenty of times? And so I also decided to take a lesson through any problem. To analyse what had happened, what part I had played, where the mistake lay. And then to alter my attitude, so that I stopped fighting life with all its painful situations and began to unite myself with it and to work for the solution of its problems. To accept what comes, what others are and what I am myself, not to go against events, but to be taught by them. To shoulder my responsibilities without groaning and without the feeling of being wronged and abandoned. This is what I did, and I never again changed my decision, that is, to make life my Master, at its every moment.

THE FIELDS

From the very first days when I went to the Society I realised that certain words were heard very frequently between the Master and the disciples. I didn't find this strange, because it is a well known fact that in any circle of people who are concerned with a specific subject, the same thing happens. From my personal experiences in the past I had known similar situations, particularly in the professional sphere. For example, when I started to work as an infant teacher, I saw that the headteacher and my other colleagues had a vocabulary of their own, which, of course, was connected with the object of our work. I had noticed the same thing in the circle of the painters I came into contact with at the time when I too was painting. Thus, my first impression from the words which I heard at the Society was neither positive or negative; I accepted them as something very natural.

As the weeks passed, this impression changed and began to turn into, first, puzzlement, and then irritation. Because, whereas in other circles the repetition of the same words was within certain reasonable bounds, at the Society, the exact opposite was true. The frequency with which a word was heard, particularly from the lips of the Master, was so great that in the end you had the feeling that this word alone was the constant subject of all the conversations, our sole interest.

The word ‘attachment’, for instance, had become our daily diet. You said something to the Master about a problem which you had and he would reply: “Attachment, Mrs Klairi”. A group would be discussing issues of discipleship, and at unexpected moments the Master would chime in with “Well, it’s attachment, you see; there it is”.

This went on for many months, but even today it recurs from time to time when a disciple is passing through a new crisis of attachment to something or other. Since disciples, particularly when they are embarking upon their work, have many dependences, the Master, by repeating this word, wishes to point the problem out to them, so they can see it and understand it. However, the issue expands further: the disciples begin to imitate the Master and to point out to one another each other's attachments. And so, in the early days, I had the impression that attachment had acquired an existence of its own and, like an unseen presence, went up and down the stairs at the Society, came in and out of the rooms, and lay in wait for the suitable individual to sit on that person's head like a bronze crown.

Another of the words which from time to time became the pivot of discussions was, in those early days, the word 'unconscious'. A disciple would be speaking, explaining a thought, or describing an incident, or simply answering a question, and the voice of the Master would suddenly be heard saying in a dismissive tone: "Unconscious". I must admit that I didn't like that word in the slightest; it was worse than attachment. Because, while I knew that human beings have many dependences – this I understood from the very first lesson – the unconscious was totally unexpected, unknown, very deeply hidden in everybody.

You speak, for example, about some conversation which you have had with your husband, and when you think you've made a very good job of it, suddenly a completely unconscious jealousy is revealed to you. You say that you have decided to change your job, because, as you maintain, your new job will be more rewarding, and a hidden fear of your present job springs out of your words.

Because the unconscious is usually negative; it conceals all those weak spots of our selves which we refuse to see, and when this word was heard on the lips of the Master, I was always flustered. "Let's see what he'll bring to light this time, what new weakness or failure of mine", I used to think. There are, of course, also positive features which man doesn't know are lying concealed within him but which take a very long time to come to the surface, and so the first unconscious items which make their appearance are mostly unwelcome and painful.

Both in the case of attachment and that of the unconscious, and in the case of other words or sentences which the Master uses very frequently at certain times, I could easily find an explanation. It was, in any case, perfectly obvious. By pointing out a problem, a situation, and by repeating the relevant word many times, he shook our consciousness in order to force us to emerge from that problem by doing the appropriate work. There was, however, one word whose meaning and the reasons why the Master said it many times a day it was impossible for me to discover. This was the word 'field'.

I had noticed that he talked about 'field' to the old disciples and to those who were completely new. He used it at moments of serious analyses or of simple sentences which had to do with everyday matters. He used it in connection with things great and small, abstract and specific, important and insignificant. Field above, field below, field to the right, field to the left. I had begun to feel positively encircled by this word, whose meaning, in any event, I hardly understood. It was as if my cells had become a field, just as my feelings had. And I saw the same thing in the others.

There were moments when I felt that I, the field, was going into the Society, meeting the disciple-fields and all together holding field discussions about the field. Until in the end everything else disappeared and the only thing left present was the field. Pure madness, so much so that I wanted to shout out: "Have words disappeared from the Greek vocabulary? We have such a rich language, why are we steamrollering it like this?" This thought, of course, didn't correspond at all to the reality, because one of the things which had impressed me from the first moment was the wealth of words which the Master used.

As to the word 'field', I will give a few examples to show what exactly was happening with this issue. I would go into the Master's room wearing a new dress, and he would say to me: "That's a very nice field, Mrs Klairi". Soon another disciple would come with an air of distress, and the Master would ask: "What field is it that you have within you?" Another would follow, bringing some work he had done, and, when we'd heard it, there would come the now familiar answer: "A correct field, that, but there are some gaps". Later, we would be discussing some sick person who had asked for help from the healing section, and when we disciples said what we thought was the cause of the illness, the Master would correct us: "No, no, the field is elsewhere". And so the dress, distress, the work, and the illness disappeared somewhere, and in their place came one thing only, the now legendary FIELD. Like an all-powerful ruler, it held the sceptres of all the teaching, and it still holds them, but in a different way now, and comes to touch our heads with its magic wand, as if we were knights who are being ennobled by the king to this office! Only we, instead of being knights, are appointed simply as fields...

I must admit that, in spite of the impression which the use of this word made on me and in spite of it being my custom to analyse everything I heard very carefully and searchingly, to begin with, I made no analysis of 'field'. The analysis came much later, when I began to discover its profound significance and to look for a global understanding of the teaching which I had received all those years with the Master. Perhaps I didn't dare at that time to see what message this word was conveying to us. Perhaps I didn't have – certainly I didn't have – the knowledge necessary to enter deeply into its meaning. In any event, little by little I became so used to it that I no longer heard it, even though its meaning had passed unconsciously within me. Like the other disciples, I myself began to use it, without thinking very much about it.

There was no danger of making any mistake, I could call anything I liked a field, without any problem. This much I had understood completely!

Today, any perplexity which I had on this matter has been resolved. The teaching which I have received has covered so many factors and has extended to so many analyses and the corresponding experiences that I can say with confidence what 'field' means, and why the Master gives it so much emphasis. Everybody speaks quite naturally about certain fields, but they do this rarely; they prefer to call things by their own individual names. If you pay attention to the speakers on television, for example, you will see that for many days on end this word is not heard. When I myself happened to hear it at an early stage, I used to laugh inwardly and think that the speakers had slipped up in the same way we did, and had fallen into the trap of the field.

But is it, in the end, a trap, or is it perhaps the opposite? Is it perhaps a loosening of bonds, a release from certain patterns of form and established states of affairs which imprison man? What is it that all of us do? We give names, we personify, we make endless classifications and separations. Not that these don't exist, certainly they exist, and, moreover, they are necessary for our communication. We can't talk about people when we call them all fields. We are obliged to use their separate name in order to understand one another. Nor is it possible to speak of distress or joy without defining them precisely as distress and joy. Because, of course, we wouldn't know what the other person was talking about if we called them all just fields.

In the light of this, the teaching 'about fields' is meaningless, or so it seems, at least. But when one has accepted the concept of the 'Master' in all its manifestations and when one has inner and empirical confirmation of the teaching as given to us by the specific Master, I can say that, on the contrary, it has a vast meaning. It serves to bring a completely different current in a world which lives in separateness, in personification, in the need to project the separate egos. As this word begins to assimilate all things with its common semantic content, classifications are reduced, oppositions are smoothed out. Perhaps it might be thought that this is a levelling out, and that no levelling out is desirable. But it isn't anything of the sort, it is a much deeper form of assimilation which has to do with the essence of phenomena and not appearance and external form.

The word 'field', according to the dictionaries, means an area of land or a notional extent of energy. For this reason it is used by physics, mathematics, and other sciences (magnetic field, field of vision, etc.). The existence of an area, however, suggests the presence of a greater area to which the previous one belongs, as far as the whole boundless extent of the universe. This applies alike to the natural world as to the inner consciousness. The fact that we all have a name, because this is necessary for us, does not cancel out the other fact – that we are, if you will, an 'extent', that is, a part only in a whole which consists of boundless things with endless names. When a Master talks to you about your feelings as fields, about your thoughts as fields, about your actions as fields, you automatically begin to wonder who in fact you are, where you belong, what is the greater consciousness which contains you. And gradually, while the small element of individuality is revealed to you, the great one, entirety, the one which encloses everything is also at the same time revealed.

But where is all this leading? Isn't it discouraging to realise how small you are, a mere dot in the universe? Yes, such a conception is in fact displeasing, if it is restricted to the physical body, to the human form alone. But it is transformed into well-being when it is extended to the conscious existence, because this does not have limitations. Consciousness is formless, and so can be contained in any natural breadth, including within a human being. The formless does not take up space, it is everywhere alike, it is the presence of God everywhere. Isn't the simple realisation of this reality true well-being?

Of course, all the things I have said about the fields all being traced back to a single field are mental analyses, and it isn't enough to understand them in order to be able to experience them immediately. The conception is one thing, and realisation another. But a step has been taken, and the action will follow, in order, over the years, for the transition from the idea to the essence of the idea to occur. What is important is the constant expansion of the self, progression towards the boundless.

And, to use the Master's words, what is important is to pass from one field to the next, until one day you arrive at a field which is no field!

CHOICES

The Master says that man can make whatever choice he wishes, he can choose, that is, what he will express, what task he will carry out, what his actions will be. Apart, naturally, from certain cases of mental impairment, everybody has freedom of choice. Because this idea is completely the opposite of the familiar views held about the various limitations on man, I asked him if we could discuss this issue. A single discussion was not enough to cover it, of course, but we reverted to the same subject very frequently from time to time, so that I could come to understand what exactly was the meaning which the Master wished to convey to me. I will give some of the findings of the dialogues which took place at various times.

"You say, Master, that there is absolute freedom of choice in man. What exactly do you mean by that?"

"I mean that if someone wants to do something, then he will undoubtedly do it, however many obstacles present themselves."

"What you say doesn't receive confirmation, because the only thing that I, for example, want is to overcome all my difficulties and to be liberated from human weaknesses. But this, at least for now, hasn't happened."

"It hasn't happened because you don't want it wholeheartedly. That is to say, although there is within you the will for it to happen, there is also another will which is still holding you captive. And this second will is, it seems, greater than the first and overrides it."

"I don't understand about this will. What is it that I want so much that I don't choose my freedom?"

"It doesn't matter what it is that you desire. It may be anything at all, for example, to be relieved of some responsibility, someone to show an interest in you, to be economically well-to-do, and so on. All these things and a thousand others come into conflict with your other desire."

"Are you saying that I shouldn't concern myself about anything; for example, that I shouldn't take care to have whatever is necessary for my family to live?"

"I didn't say anything like that. You should take proper care about everything. The issue is from what position you do it. If your primary will is, as you said, your spiritual liberation, then in working for all the other things, you must remain free, whatever those other things are. For example, you are to look after your body, your house, and so on, but don't look upon these things as something different from freedom."

"I understand what you are saying, but there are also obstacles which are insuperable, illnesses, family situations, and many other things."

"I would say that these exist, but also that they don't exist. Because it has been proved that people with illnesses have succeeded by their will in overcoming their illnesses. And if not all of them have done this, some of them have been able to achieve a spiritual serenity within their sick body. And then, we have the examples of those who were born into poor families and by their will have become extremely rich. How do all these things come about? It is simply a matter of choice, of decision, and of work."

"You said before that I may have a desire to be economically well-off which is limiting me. Now you express your admiration for certain poor people who have become rich. In the end, what is this need, positive or negative?"

"It's neither the one nor the other. It is simply a need. If, however, it is stopping you – when you have another will – from expressing it, then it's limiting. But for someone who wants only what he is doing, whatever that is, it isn't a limitation, it's an expression of his will."

"If we look at things in this way, we would say that someone who kills is doing the right thing, since his will is to be a murderer."

"No, here we are going on to another issue. Murder, like any other crime, is something which infringes the rights of others, or the laws of nature. There is no field of choice in such matters."

"Very well, let's leave crimes aside. But what do you say about a man who is jealous of his wife? Isn't he infringing in this way some of her rights, since he distresses her with his attitude?"

"Jealousy, Mrs Klairi, is not a matter of choice. It is due to man's ignorance of his inner powers; as he's not aware of these, he doesn't know how to control his emotions. So he abandons himself to the current of the jealousy which floods him and dominates him."

"And so a choice without knowledge isn't possible, according to what you are saying. But which people have this knowledge?"

"It isn't necessary that there should be this knowledge which you speak of; this is a matter for those who wish to acquire self-knowledge, to express their will for spiritual development. Everybody has desires, but they also have the potential of the will to fulfil them. If a woman decides to become a mother and by her will works to be as good a mother as she can, then there is no problem, or any conflict with other wills. Because stability in the task which she has chosen to carry out gives her calm, it expresses her fully. The problem begins when there are vacillations between two or more wills."

"Let's say, now, Master, that someone wishes to choose what he is going to do in life, but doesn't know what exactly he wants. Where can he find what expresses him? Are there really so many choices? I know people have chosen something which they didn't want and have been forced to spend their whole life in a mistake. Why does that happen?"

"I will give you an example. Let's say that a friend of yours invites you to a meal, and that there you see a large table with a great many dishes of food. But you fill your plate with one kind of food only, either because you like it or because you can't be bothered to go round and round the table, or because you are afraid to try new tastes. Who is responsible for your choice? Naturally, you are; it is you who have confined yourself for some reason to one kind of food only."

"I can't connect this example completely with the issue under discussion. Are you telling me, in other words, that it's as easy to find all the ideas for all our decisions as it is to find different dishes on the table? But where are all these ideas and wills? I don't understand this."

"But they're all within you. In our mind are all the ideas which we can make into reality. All that is required is that we should not close this mind, that we should let it receive everything freely, and then what it is that we want to do on each occasion will be found. But if the mind is dominated by one thought only, often an obsessive one, then what happened in the example occurs: the plate is filled with one kind of food only."

"Yes, but to follow this line of thought, that there is no limitation, by leaving my mind open to everything, I could say, for example, that I want to be a man, or that I want to be 30 years younger. But these things can't happen, even if there is a great will for them."

"Man has to follow the natural laws, and for that reason he can't do the things you mention. These laws are a protection for himself, necessary for the whole of humanity at the level of evolution which it is currently at. But we have examples of people with greater spiritual evolution who, as you yourself have read, have been able to transcend even physical bounds. It is a proven fact that initiates can renew their cells, so that their bodies remain forever young, if this is required for the service which they perform. Also, as we can read in the biography of Ramakrishna, that great saint brought about changes in his body, he developed breasts and had periods. This phenomenon was also studied by the doctors of the time. We also know that there are people who can hover in the air, thus transcending the laws of gravity, and others who don't need food, since they assimilate directly the rays of the sun. But none of this has to do with our discussion; I've told you this simply for you to see that where there is true will, there are no obstacles. The issue of choice which should concern a disciple is, however, totally different. The disciple is not an initiate, nor is he a saint, even though he is being taught how to, one day, reach that level. Nor should he be concerned with certain spectacular accomplishments, such as, for example, learning to fly. We're talking about another choice here."

"What, in the end, is this choice? Can you please summarise this?"

"We shall set, first of all, two things as a condition for telling you what freedom of choice means. The first is that the people we are talking about must have developed a consciousness of themselves, they must know, very simply, that there is a certain power within them, and that if this is encouraged by their will, then they can go ahead with the realisation of what they want. We are not talking either about under-age individuals, nor about those who are mentally impaired, but about a normal adult. The second condition is that we shall confine ourselves within the natural laws which we all know and which, as we have said, are a protection for man. In the light of this there is only one choice: between evolution and stagnation. If a person wishes to evolve in any sphere (professional, economic, family, social, personal), then he expresses the will for this evolution. If, however, he wants to stay where he is, then his decision in favour of being static will be expressed accordingly, again in those areas we have spoken of, or in many others."

"And how is it that all the special issues which you have spoken of are included in one choice only? Isn't it a different thing for someone to become a businessman from becoming a dancer?"

"Yes, certainly it is, but in the one case and in the other, deep down, the choice is one. It is simply manifested through another pattern. And this choice is between the will to do something and the will not to do it. What is of primary importance is the will to achieve something, and then the path for the expression comes later."

"And if an individual wants to do many things, what happens then?"

"It's the same again. The same will is channelled to the one or to the many. There are famous painters who were also scientists and fathers of families. Things don't conflict with one another when they are directed by the one will, which simply manifests itself in many ways."

"And what does the Master want for his disciples?"

"The Master doesn't want anything, because for the Master, all the wills of the disciples go back to this one will. Each disciple has a right to express himself in whatever way he chooses. But the Master hopes that the choice of all the disciples will be their evolution, spirituality, union with the will of God."

"Thank you, Master, for all this analysis."

MEDITATION

"Meditation is life, it is healing, it is revelation. It revitalises man, expands the consciousness, brings about union with all things. Meditation is well-being and illumination." This is the way that Masters who teach it speak of meditation – but also disciples who are taught it.

The words sound like exaggeration, and very often they are misinterpreted. At other times they influence people to such an extent that they attempt to learn to meditate on their own. But without the guidance of a Master or of some advanced disciple, the results will not come, and, moreover, this may lead to exactly the opposite, negative, situations. Because during meditation the soul's energies and powers are revitalised within man, they strengthen him and veritably flood him. For the correct distribution and utilisation of these powers there must be a guide, someone with knowledge. For this reason, although I shall speak here about meditation, I shall only give as much detail as I think is without danger for the reader, who may not have any experience or knowledge of this particular matter.

My personal view, confirmed by innumerable experiences in meditation – both my own and those of other disciples – is that meditation reveals miracle. The miracle of life, and of death. The miracle of the boundless and of the particle. The miracle within what is beautiful and ugly, within eternity and the moment.

I was so totally ignorant of spiritual matters when I started out on my discipleship, as I have said, but I was also so much thirsting for a deeper knowledge of myself, that I accepted immediately the lesson on meditation, without any reaction against it whatsoever. I didn't know what it was, I didn't expect anything preconceived from it, I had no fear about what might happen to me. So I handed myself over completely to the guidance which I received, without thoughts and emotions which would hinder abandonment to what was happening. Perhaps this absolute receptiveness helped those results to occur which began to come every day and to surprise me.

Surprise, wonder, revelation! This was what I experienced in meditation from the very first days of my discipleship. Things which were incomprehensible to me occurred at that time. Incomprehensible but marvellous, and so I persevered in my work. I was seeking new experiences, I was seeking new patterns, ideas, experiences in meditation. And the Master, seeing my great need and aptitude, responded to this. For the first two or three years, he followed my daily work on meditation and every so often he would give me a new theme for me to work upon. Later, when I had established myself as a person who meditates, he left me free and simply gave me certain guidelines at rare intervals.

I call meditation a revelation of miracle because what other name could I give to the things which happened through it? Isn't the revelation of the capability of man to be able to see the internal organs of the body a miracle? Isn't it a miracle to feel all the cells revitalised and pulsating in his body? Isn't it a miracle for him to conceive with his mind ideas and very specific knowledge of things which he has never heard of in his life? Isn't it a miracle for him to be flooded by a current of power and love which he had never realised exists in the world - or in himself?

Every day a new surprise! This was what meditation was for me in the early stage of my discipleship. Even now, after ten years of daily work, there are certain times when an unexpected new feature, a new revelation comes. But now that I know that anything can happen when you are meditating, I am no longer surprised; the profound awe which I feel for the inner world of man, for the indescribable self which constantly unfolds before me and permeates the whole of me simply increases.

The revelation of miracle began from the very first day of my learning process. I remember that the Master, without explaining to me what would happen, told me simply to sit motionless, to close my eyes, and to imagine a light above my head was little by little flooding the whole of me. A lightning change then occurred in my body; it was as if great currents of energy were passing through me. And then, still with his guidance, I began to see, literally, to 'see', all my internal organs. This was followed by many other occurrences which I shall not give an account of here, since, in any event, in the book on Spiritual Healing I have described this meditation in detail. In connection with what followed a little later, the most important things were the realisation of the flow of energy in the body and the revelation of the possibility of inner vision. These things were more than enough to establish me immediately as a 'meditator'. I would say that I had received a baptism within my very self.

I left a little later to return home. I was so astonished by what had happened that I felt dizzy. But I never imagined that I would have this experience repeatedly – and, moreover, very soon. When I had done the necessary jobs and talked a little with my family, I went to bed in order to calm down. I fell asleep at the usual time while I was still thinking of my experience of that afternoon, but without any longer feeling the powerful current which had flooded me earlier. This had disappeared completely.

But suddenly something happened while I was asleep, and I woke up. I opened my eyes abruptly; it was as though a strange unknown power had shaken me. I looked at the clock. Three in the morning! I looked at my husband, but I saw that he was sleeping undisturbed next to me. I then noticed that my hand was resting on his back. While I was attempting to understand what had happened, a voice in my mind said to me urgently: “Love him”. Before I had time to understand what was happening, that same current which I had experienced in the afternoon again unexpectedly flooded me, and its power accumulated in the hand which was resting on my husband. I had the feeling that my hand was made entirely of light, and, without thinking what I was doing, I allowed the light and the power to pass into his body. I was certain that at that moment I gave to him the power which had been given to me, I conveyed to him the current of life, even if he didn’t realise it because he was asleep.

This event was forgotten among so many new and unexpected things which happened to me each day. I didn’t concern myself with it, nor did the Master give me any explanation when I told him about it. In any event, I think that I may not have understood at that time the significance of it, and perhaps, moreover, it would have given rise to some confusion for me. The conclusion which I have reached today about this particular episode, and about everything that happens to a disciple, as I have said, is that all Masters have as their aim to make the disciple conscious of the inner Master. Every lesson, every meditation, even every simple piece of advice on their part has this objective: that the consciousness of man should rise up. The first current which I experienced was also the first awakening which occurred within me. The inner Master, whom I was so much seeking after, revived with the help of the Master and began to guide me day and night. An example of his guidance was that first order to me to love human beings, as well as what he indicated to me about the way of expressing love, that is, the transference of energy from my body to theirs.

In the years which followed I became increasingly aware of the importance of the inner Master who rises up chiefly with the help of meditation. I will give certain examples from my personal experiences, without speaking of methods of meditation, which, as I have said, should not be used by those who are not receiving proper guidance as to their use. It will be apparent in these examples that human consciousness within man is boundless and covers everything, from the smallest to the greatest of all.

I remember that on one occasion, when I was thinking about the expanse of the created world and trying to study it mentally with the facts which are to be found in books, I brought this subject to my mind when I was meditating. Although I had had many confirmations of the possibilities of meditation, nevertheless I could never have expected or imagined what happened.

As my mind was focused on the infinite, on the inconceivable concept of expanse, I suddenly realised that I had started to expand. It was as though I was growing, I was taking on other dimensions, I was losing my limits. This feeling was so clear that I felt my body to see if I had really grown and expanded. No, my body was as it always was, something else was expanding within me – the mind, the consciousness, the spirit! I let myself see what would happen, and little by little I began to take on a consciousness of the whole of the planet, the solar system, the galaxy. I was constantly spreading out, and the expansion of the mind didn't seem to have an end or a beginning. But what was happening was not only an indeterminate feeling, but, on the contrary, a perfectly clear inner vision. I 'saw' – and I had no doubt about this – the whole of creation! My mind had transcended every limit. But I knew that this mind, although it was mine, was another existence, an ontological existence which cannot be described. And, quite simply, this entity was looking at its own creation! The spectacle was magnificent.

A whole universe. Boundless suns with many planets. And others with only one or two. Red, green, yellow, golden, and white suns. Suns near and far, small and great. Stars innumerable. Sections of void between all the heavenly bodies. And far distant, cloud formations which travelled as groups and passed in between the suns. Unlooked-for waves of luminous energy, which like fiery snakes rushed into infinity and disappeared. Vibrations, movements, revolutions, one life which pulsated as a whole and advanced into space. My breath had been taken away by my amazement at the variety and the ceaseless movement. And then I saw the whole universe rushing into chaos. Like a spiral cone, with an unimaginably powerful centre which advanced with enormous impetus, carrying behind it the more scattered points of its spiral. And as it entered the chaos, new suns were created there, new galaxies made their appearance. I was literally enchanted. I felt completely at a loss in the face of this indescribable expanse. And I stayed there, in the universe, for a long time, in a state of ecstasy. Later, little by little, my consciousness returned to the natural plane and I opened my eyes. Meditation had given me the answer I was looking for – and much more comprehensively than I had expected.

Other disciples tell of similar experiences. However, experiences of such a kind cannot always be confirmed by some kind of proof or by specific items of knowledge. A person who has these experiences doesn't doubt what he sees and what happens, but much time and much more tangible examples are needed before he is firmly established in his belief in the capability of the mind to cover everything and in the profound importance of meditation. This is why the Master advises us when we are meditating on something specific to check everything that is revealed to us against information to be found in books or which is proved directly in life. Proof also brings with it firm grounding in a belief in meditation.

In order for me to be established in this belief, it was necessary to pass through many specific meditation processes which gave me the certainty that the things which I saw were not an error, however strange and unlikely they seemed to me. To make this truth apparent, I will give an entirely different example which proves that the things which come in meditation are correct. This was a very simple happening. There was in our house an ashtray which was used by my husband when he was watching television. This ashtray was suddenly lost, and for two days I looked for it in vain. On the third morning I sat down to meditate, as always, on the settee; there was no thought in my mind about the ashtray. However, completely without warning, as had happened with the meditation on the universe, my mind expanded again, and I then saw all the objects in the room, even though my eyes were, of course, closed. I also saw that underneath the settee, at the back and near the wall, was the lost ashtray. I got up at once, pulled out the settee, and there, in fact, the ashtray was waiting for me! Confirmation had come, as, in any event, it comes to many disciples, when they meditate on specific subjects. From that day forward, I have never been distracted by thoughts of doubt or disbelief as to the truth which is taught by meditation.

It is, of course, very natural that there should be doubts in those who practise meditation, particularly at the beginning of the learning process. This is because, apart from the objects in the natural field, other things, often with absolutely no connection with reality, project themselves. Strange forms, scenes, and happenings which don't occur in life, transformations of beings, incomprehensible concepts, and so on. All these things are reminiscent of certain dreams which cannot be explained, as if they happen in some other dimension. But everything is explained, as I came to understand, little by little – with the help of the Master when the person meditating cannot find their interpretation on his own.

I can now reply with certainty to beginners, who often ask the question: "Is it possible that all this that happens to me in meditation isn't true?" It's all true, but there is a difference in the manner of presentation or in the proportion of this truth. Depending upon the level of evolution of the disciple, on his true aptitude and his preparatory work in meditation, the reply emerges on corresponding scales. The ways vary, just as the methods of teaching pupils in a school vary. Children in an infants' school are taught certain moral principles through tales, so that their interest is aroused. But when they are old enough, the same principles are given to them by examples and rules, and later, in adolescence, by means of their totally analytical meaning. The same thing happens in meditation. For as long as the disciple needs symbols, which are frequently reminiscent of fairy tales, these are projected by the inner Master. Later, he passes on to deeper analyses, advancing to the field of the mind more and more substantively. If it were not like this, knowledge would not come, because of the impossibility of understanding at the various stages of discipleship.

I can remember that in the first year, I saw many symbols in my meditation, often incomprehensible ones. One day, when I wanted to understand what wisdom is and how man can comprehend it, I saw in my meditation a venerable, aged figure, who radiated love and profound knowledge. The body was that of a man on the right-hand side and of a woman on the left. This, of course, bore no relation to reality. Such human beings do not exist on our planet, except for some very rare exceptions of evolved beings who, as we have said, have the power to intervene in their gender and to change it at will.

I looked in astonishment at this aged figure, and many thoughts passed through my mind: "Was it perhaps some kind of monster? Perhaps this being wasn't wise. How is it possible for a body to be at one and the same time both male and female?" I was ready to stop the meditation, but something held me motionless, something which I saw in this strange figure. I had all around me a radiance, an expression of holiness and boundless peace. I felt that it was radiating love and knowledge. So I stayed to see this wise being for as long as its presence was before me. At the end, it made a gesture of blessing with its right hand, and then disappeared. I continued to meditate, in order to find a rational explanation of the phenomenon, so as to be able to relate it to my initial question – as to what wisdom means. The figure certainly exuded wisdom, but why was it formed in this way? However much I searched for the answer, the answer did not come. I was lacking some very important item of knowledge, and I couldn't find it.

The next day I sought the help of the Master, and he told me that the symbol which I had seen was a very substantive lesson which I had received from the inner Master. He explained that every human being conceals within him all the opposing powers of life, and is, so to speak, a hermaphrodite in a spiritual field. Wisdom manifests itself only when man has harmonised all these powers within himself and begins to express them in his life. As long as he separates them and restricts them, they don't express themselves. He added that these powers are strength, will, love, and knowledge. Because in the natural field powers are personified by the two genders, the symbol which I had seen wished to show me how the harmonisation of opposites is an expression of wisdom. When I asked why I had seen this figure, he replied that this had come because at that time I was not able to receive the message of the teaching in any other way. The symbolism was striking and it stirred my curiosity to go ahead with a larger search, whereas an intellectual analysis would not have helped me at that time; it would have tired me, or I would not have understood it. The whole of this conversation confirmed for me yet again the wisdom of the inner Master.

As time passed, I noticed that all the disciples have the tendency to meditate on matters of lofty concepts, moral principles, holy entities, and so on. There is an inherent refusal to enter more deeply into anything which seems to them negative. The Master, however, wishes to break down one-sidedness in their preferences and recommends to them that meditation should be on all matters, globally.

Once a disciple asked the Master:

"Master, on what should I meditate?"

"On whatever you like", he answered.

"So the subjects should not be only the good, love, faith, or even a beautiful object, such as, for example, a rose?"

"Not only. You can meditate on all the opposites of the things you have mentioned."

"But then I may be influenced by them."

"You won't be influenced if you reflect during meditation that all things are the creation of God, that all things are in the light, and that in all things there is the spiritual essence. Then meditation will be without danger."

"And what is the benefit of entering more deeply into negative things?"

"From your question it seems that you have a problem with the negative. But if you meditated on this in the right way, then you would be relieved of the problem, because it will be revealed to you that in everything God, who is everywhere present, is concealed. This realisation alone helps the so-called 'bad' things to be differentiated, to become the 'good'."

Influenced by the Master's words, I decided to enter more deeply into negative things, to see what positive findings I would have. I chose two completely opposed subjects, so that my work would be more objective. The first concerned a frequent problem of relationships: why a man and a woman with entirely different characters and psychology decide to get married. The second was a natural object, more specifically: faeces. Meditation on these things – normally considered 'negative' – gave me new revelations, as if my mind was receiving some stimuli unknown to me up to then. Dynamic stimuli, which began to dissolve within me established ideas about good and bad, pleasant and unpleasant.

The couple whom I decided to investigate were friends of mine. I knew the personalities of the two individuals very well. The woman was a dynamic, demonstrative person with many interests and social relations. The man was quiet, he worked calmly, avoided having many contacts, he was what we call a withdrawn person. These contrasts caused constant friction between them, as the one tried to impose upon the other his or her own way of life.

When I began this meditation, I expected that I would see exactly the same characteristics in the energy field, that is, in the way in which the energies and powers of the individuals flowed in their bodies. But as I entered more deeply into them, I was astonished. The opposite of what I expected was the case. The woman had many withholdings of energy at many points of the body, particularly in the solar plexus, in the area of the abdomen, which is the seat of the emotions. The man, on the other hand, showed a much better flow and distribution of the energies in his body. This seemed to me inexplicable, unbelievable. How can someone who is closed in upon himself not withhold his powers, and, on the other hand, how can someone who is demonstrative have energy charges?

I had spent a long time on this study when suddenly, as I was focused on the dark solar plexus of the woman, I saw great currents of power being emitted from within it. And then I understood. The woman was engaged in constant activity precisely because there were so many accumulations within her, so that every so often they made her wish to discharge them by means of all her concerns. The man, however, had no such need, because by spreading, to a large degree, his energy equally throughout the whole of the body, he found relief simply and only by this function.

When I had received this surprising answer, I tried to find out why the two had married. Again I brought them mentally before me and saw that there was a great attraction between them.

The flow in the body of the man magnetised the accumulated energy of the woman, and vice versa. For the first time I understood what is meant when they say that opposites attract one another. The attraction was not between the personalities, which came into constant conflict, but between the powers of the soul, which helped one another by balancing their different flows. It was as if someone had told me a very great secret, as if I had been initiated into a deep level of knowledge.

However, I didn't stop this meditation here, because I wanted to see how two such souls decided upon marriage, since they don't know that they complement one another. People see chiefly the personality, and not the manifestations of the soul, as these are apparent in the energy field. So why had our friends married? At this point, another unexpected thing occurred. I felt myself encircled by an unseen presence, which was at the same time also encircling the couple. This presence, entirely formless, was the source of the energies in the couple, and as the source, seemed to be directing the lesser powers within them. I would say that it was prompting the two individuals to unite, to become one. I realised that the unseen presence was the consciousness, the inner Master, who knew the needs of the souls and gave them the appropriate partner.

A fullness then engulfed me, a sense of certainty, as if all my fears had left me. Because how can you be afraid when you know that some higher self is watching over everything? Even if you have to go through disagreements with your partner, to have problems and conflicts, doesn't all of this fade before the magic of the knowledge which is guiding you? If we all knew what is hidden within phenomena, then we should be calm and we would simply accept the obstacles as an apprenticeship of our soul. It was with this thought that I completed the meditation, because I had understood that within the 'bad' – the couple's problems – wisdom, love, union were concealed.

As to the meditation on the faeces, I will speak only of certain features of this experience. Because the subjects which came as a revelation on that day cannot be given for the present, as they concern other fields of the learning process. The procedure started with the reflection that I was next to a pile of faeces and I was looking at them. Immediately their odour surrounded me, as if they were really next to me, and, surprised by this, I felt the usual revulsion for them. However, when I reflected that the pure spiritual essence is also within them, my distaste began to grow less, and I began to accept the odour, and then I was able to go more deeply into the subject.

I observed that in the atoms of the matter there was a movement, like certain minor powers trying to separate themselves from the heap, and that the odour was due to their great friction. As the faeces began to dry out with their dissolution and decomposition, I remembered immediately the importance of manure, which is necessary for plants. In this way I realised that the odour, a derivative of the process of decomposition, served the purpose of transforming the waste into food. I saw that through a constant movement, it brought about, by recycling, a new form. If, then, the odour, the repulsive characteristic of faeces, is a necessary condition for the positive result, then it seems that even in this, good, wisdom is latent. In comparing this odour with various negative characteristics of human beings, I began to try to find out what happens when these manifest themselves. Naturally, I saw that these too cause a revulsion in others, but if, for example, I as a disciple accept their expression as a process which will bring out the good from within them, then certainly I won't feel bad when these are put forward.

The study of negative characteristics went on for some time. When I was objective in deepening my approach and managed to overcome my revulsion for them, I always came to the same conclusion: that in the depths of the most evil, unpleasant, painful thing there is the purpose of the good, the manifestation of the universal consciousness.

As will be clear from what I have said, meditation shows the miracle of life. It reveals mysteries, opens up new horizons in man. As the body is activated, the miracle also occurs in the person who is meditating. The cells are revitalised and he acquires new powers in the whole of his being. I shall never forget the feeling caused by my own body, which very soon I experienced as ten years younger. And my brain also worked at a different rate, as if it had been rid of murky and dark ideas. Even my expression became different, as I was told by those who hadn't seen me for some time. Little by little, the person who meditates learns to know the energies and the powers of the soul and to direct them by his will in the body and in the energy centres. In this way he learns to transform the passions and the desires into love and creativity. Isn't it remarkable that yogis of a very great age have amazing good health and retain in the body a youthful vigour? And this of course is due to the constant work of meditation which they do and to the eradiation which they emit to humanity.

The Master, with his knowledge of the value of meditation, urges his disciples to meditate constantly, all day, even when they are at work, and not to limit themselves only to certain regular times for this. He says that the whole of mankind meditates, but doesn't do so consciously. Because every mental process, every dialogue, even every action is a form of meditation, since in all these things there is a recycling of energy from one thing to another. The disciple should do what everybody does – but consciously and always with reference to a wider field of consciousness. He should seek, that is to say, as at the time of normal meditation, union with a field of the inner Master, who is knowledge and light, and through this union live simply all the activities of the day. When this is done regularly, then the disciple advances in his spiritual progress, which is always progress within a more expanded consciousness.

The subject of meditation is a vast, multifarious, and composite one. It cannot be explained in a single chapter – or in a single book, I would say. In my file I have written down a great many experiences in meditation and on different mental levels on many topics; I shall revert to these where necessary in the chapters which follow. In concluding this first presentation on meditation, I would like to repeat what the Masters say: that meditation means life, revelation, well-being, deliverance!

BALANCING OF OPPOSITES

Before I began to meditate on the subject of the negative and to accept that, deep down, that too is positive, I had the greatest objections when the Master gave me a lesson in this connection. I can remember that the first time that he dealt with this topic, I was beside myself. "What are you saying, Master?" I asked him. "That I should love malice, pain, ugliness? Impossible. I hate these things and shall go on hating them until I die." He calmly replied: "But as long as you hate them, these things will torment you, you won't be liberated." "Let them torment me as much as they like. I tell you again: it's out of the question that I should love the thief, the jealous person, the miser. Don't tell me anything again on this issue." I got up and went away from him, as though he was unbalanced, mentally sick. Have you ever heard of such a thing? That you should love evil, he says. I wonder what this person's going to teach us next.

The Master would revert to the same subject in various ways which proved what he said. One day he told us a story. There was, he told us, a saint who had a brother. This brother was killed by a certain thief. The thief, terrified when they found him out and wanted to arrest him, entered the saint's house. The saint, instead of giving him up to his pursuers, hid him under his mantle and so saved him from certain condemnation. The magnanimity of the saint made such an impression on the murderer that from that moment he was a changed man; he became honest and good.

This story is impressive, and it shows how love dissolves hate and transforms it into goodness. But I didn't feel ready even to begin to attempt anything of the kind. In any event, I reflected, I wasn't a saint. What saints do cannot be done by ordinary people.

The months passed, and the subject of the rejection of the negative recurred every so often. With it, however, also came its opposite: the need for the positive, about which all the disciples took the same view – all of them wanted it and desired it. But since life does not have in store only pleasant things, very often there were difficulties and disappointments, which gave rise to the familiar human mood changes. The Master always spoke of the deliverance which man experiences when he learns not to oscillate between the one and the other, but look upon both in the same way.

In a group lesson, he told us the following: "The life of man is a progression along a razor's edge. In order to advance, he must keep a perfect balance, so as not to fall to right or left, to be steady, not to be distracted, to look constantly ahead, to his goal. But until he learns how to progress, he falls and gets up again many times. The disciple is trained by the Master to balance the opposing powers which lead him astray, precisely as an acrobat does; to maintain a stability in his step, but also to be at the same time flexible, that is, to be constantly on the alert, so as to manage the opposing forces of life. Discipleship is precisely this practice in balancing."

"Here we go again", I thought. "He'll tell us now that we must look upon good and bad in the same way. How insistent he is sometimes. Nothing can change him." I didn't speak, because the very thought of love for the bad disturbed me deeply. I waited for someone else to ask the question. In fact, a disciple asked what the opposing forces of life are which must be balanced. And I waited, ready to explode as soon as he gave the familiar answer. But he said something else – entirely unexpected. He said only two words: "Attraction and repulsion". The floodgates of the disciples questions were opened. "Attraction by what, repulsion towards what? And why shouldn't there be attraction and repulsion? How can they not exist when some things are beautiful and others ugly?"

The Master then embarked upon an analysis of these forces and of the way in which they influence the functioning of man, bringing about falls and imbalance: "Man is attracted by certain things and repels others. Attraction is desire, and repulsion is refusal. These two opposing forces flood man, seeking to express themselves through him. Their power is so great that they – sometimes one and sometimes the other – pass into his mind, dominate him, and seem to become his guides. When man is distracted by a force, when, for example, he wants something very much, he doesn't see the other side: that in this way he doesn't want something else. But since refusal, whose strength is equal to that of desire, also seeks to be manifested equally by man, it invades him and the vacillations begin, balance is lost, and the fall comes."

At this point, a disciple interrupted him: "Do you mean that these forces are not a personal matter, that we don't create them on our own? But if that is the case, that man is at their mercy, he can't do anything, since they 'flood' him, as you said. So what is man's role?"

The Master replied: “It has to be understood that nothing is personal, no force, no idea, no situation. All these are fields of the Entity, everything is diffused everywhere, and, naturally, passes into man. Now, as far as man’s role is concerned, this is very substantive. Man is called upon to get to know the forces of life and to learn to balance them, because it is only thus that he will be liberated from their opposing flows. Then he will know and dominate them. He will ‘weigh up’ things; he will bring about an alignment, as happens with a pair of scales. Let’s have a look at the inner significance of this symbol. For the scales to balance absolutely, the weight and the counterweight must be equal. If it isn’t, the horizontal inclines to one side and so the cross pattern is lost, and this has to exist if we are to have a knowledge of the exact weight of every object which we weigh. The cross – as is self-evident – is formed in the scales by the vertical axis and the horizontal arms from which the pans hang. If now we relate the scales to the functioning of the disciple, we see again what I said to you before, that the disciple must be steady like the vertical axis, but be on the alert, that is, he must play with the forces, as the arms play in the scale, until the weights are balanced.”

“But it isn’t the same thing, Master”, a disciple said. “It isn’t the same thing at all to weigh a kilo of currants, putting the weight on the scale which is required, and to weight a desire which you have against the equal and opposite non-desire. Because when you want something, you want it, you can't not want it."

And another added: "And then desires and revulsions are often unexpected. You see something and you long for it, without having time to understand what's happening to you. Or, at other times, you dislike a person and you don't know why, but you don't want to start to like him. What happens in such cases?"

The Master replied that these things happen because the disciple does not always have his eye steadily on the goal. He said that if a tightrope-walker doesn't look ahead – to the end of the rope, which he must reach – but looks sometimes up and sometimes down, then he'll fall off the rope, he will have failed as an acrobat. And in this way the disciple who loses his goal fails.

Of course, naturally enough, the group asked with one voice what is, or what should be, the goal of the disciple. So then the Master said: "You know the goal of the disciple, it is that which I say to everyone all the time from the first lesson. The fact that you are now asking me the same thing again shows that you refuse to accept it, and it is for that reason, in any case, that you continue to have fluctuations. You are not looking ahead; you are looking at your desires and your refusals. And because you are looking at these, they naturally distract you. There is only one aim, it is the Entity, the union of man with the higher self. The task of the disciple is the task of the self: the emergence of power, knowledge, and love."

No one had any reply to give to these words, because we all knew very well that we departed from our goal many times a day. We are forgetful amid everyday events, we are distracted by these, we pass through endless fluctuations. The few months of our discipleship had not yet made us strong enough to govern the forces within us. In order to help us, the Master told us to study by meditation the subject of opposites, to observe our self – how and when it is led astray by something – and to discuss the results of our work in a few days.

In spite of all my objections to this specific lesson, I was forced to accept that the Master was right to some extent. Because when I disliked something, I didn't feel good, nor, again, did I feel calm when I longed for something excessively. On the contrary, I felt enslaved, or even powerless. There was no balance or peace within me. These thoughts tormented me very much, and, in order to find a way out, I began to observe the natural world and to study various laws of nature. The first thing that came into my mind was our solar system and how it works. As we all know, this system moves and exists through the absolute balance of the sun's gravitational force, which attracts the planets into the sun's sphere, and its opposite, the centrifugal force, which repels the planets from its sphere. These two forces together maintain a fixed distance between these heavenly bodies. If, for any reason, these forces lost their balance, the planets would collide with the sun, or would be scattered in space. I saw, quite simply, that the life of our solar system is based on the mutual cancellation of the force of attraction and the centrifugal force. There would be no life, at least as we know it, if one of these gained the upper hand over the other.

This first mental work didn't satisfy me completely, because I hadn't understood what exactly happens with the sun, for it to maintain the balance. This topic, compared with human powers, was a very broad one, and I couldn't make the correlations. And so I wanted to continue my research, and I was in a constant state of watchfulness, in order to find the answer. One day when I was sitting on the beach and looking at the sky, a seagull caught my interest. I saw it flying, or, rather, gliding with its wings completely motionless, looking for the sea, so that it could catch a fish. It seemed to have been stabilised at a certain height and there was no need for it to make any movement.

As I looked at it, I saw that, although it was in a horizontal position, its body and its wings formed a cross. Thus its balance was due to the stability of this position. I remembered the Master's words, which were confirmed for me at that moment by the flight of a bird. Isn't it truly remarkable that a natural law may also cover other levels of life? I wondered, however, what would happen if the seagull began to lose height. Would it continue to be in the same posture? In fact, at a certain point, a slight breeze got up, which seemed to be pushing it downwards. Immediately, it made three quick movements and went back up to where it was before, where it again immobilised its wings. Amazing! Its instinct kept it on the alert; it led it sometimes to move its wings and sometimes to leave them motionless. In this way, whatever happened, the gull remained at the height it wished, so that at some point it could reach its goal, which was its food: the fish in the sea. It knew, I would say, how to handle two opposing situations: motionlessness in the atmosphere and the movement of the wind.

In a corresponding field, man also, if he is alert and doesn't alter his goal, can have balance and can avoid being made to fall by the forces which surround him with their opposing manifestations.

Completely satisfied with this conception, I went into the water to cool down. A little further out to sea there was a boat with a fisherman in it. It seems that he had finished his work and was heading for the shore. He was rowing steadily with both hands, holding a straight course. But at certain moments a wave would strike the boat, he would row with one oar only, bring the craft straight again, and then continue on his way with both oars. In this virtually automatic action of the fisherman I saw again the same answer as I had received from the seagull. His goal was the shore, and to arrive there he had an equal sharing out of his power to the two oars, but if a current pulled him to one side, then he would apply more of his power to one of the two and so his course remained steady. Stability in aiming for the goal, alertness to the management of the currents!

When I went more deeply in meditation into the issue of balance, I saw that the waves strengthened depending upon the strength of the wind. However, the waves symbolise the emotions, the constant fluctuations of the emotional field. The wind, again, symbolises the thoughts, the specific ideas of the mind. That is to say, it is the thoughts which affect the emotion of man and make him stumble, just as the wind causes waves. So in order to rule over his emotions, he must apply a force which will differentiate the thoughts, which will balance what comes with its opposite. If he abandons himself to their current, if he forgets and is swept along by its impetus, he misses his goal – whatever that is. But is it possible that the mind is responsible for all our problems, since through it so many revelations have been made and so many means of expression of man have been found?

As I didn't find an answer to my new question, I sought the help of the Master, and he said: "The mind is, we could say, completely empty, void of ideas and thoughts. Consequently, whatever idea comes into it, it is this that it processes and develops. If the idea is positive, a positive result will come; if it is negative, naturally, the result will also be negative."

I then asked him: "If the mind is a receiver of all these ideas, as you say, who then can intervene and guide it as to which idea to develop? Is there anything more powerful than the mind?"

"Of course there is, and this is the will of man and his power. Man, over and above the specific mind of which we are all aware, is also a spiritual nature, absolute clarity. He is, we could say, another, boundless, mind, a spirit without limitations."

"But how, Master, can an individual, even if he is a disciple, intervene in the pure mind of which you speak, given that he is not aware of it? Isn't it natural for him to be distracted by what we could call the lower mind?"

"That's why I told you, Mrs Klairi, that the goal of the disciple must be union with his higher self, which is also the pure mind which I am speaking of."

"And until he arrives there, what will be happening?"

"Quite simply, he will be advancing. But the closer he comes to his goal, the fewer the fluctuations will be, because he will see the truth with increasing clarity. Isn't it like this with everything? As long as we are a long way from things, they seem hazy and confused, but the closer they get, we gain a more and more clear picture, we realise what they really are."

When I thought about this dialogue, I saw that at some point my objections had not been met. And so then I asked: "That's all very well, but in what way is balance kept? And if, again, we say that it doesn't matter how long it takes for us to gain our goal, what happens in the meantime, how does progression continue, since the opposing currents continue to affect the disciple?"

"But you yourself have given the answer with what you said previously. It's simple. Whenever an idea overwhelms you and causes intense thoughts, whether positive or negative, then you will call to your mind the exact opposites, and so you will maintain the balance."

"Ah! Now, Master, you have confused me completely. You've been telling us for so long to have positive thoughts about everything, and now you maintain that even the positive can bring about a lack of balance. I don't understand anything!"

The Master closed his eyes, and was sunk in thought for some minutes. Then he replied: "The Master says that what concerns us is balance. That is why I always say that disciples should have positive thoughts about everything, because most people do precisely the opposite, they think negatively about life, about their relationships, about events. A positive thought, then, brings the necessary balance. However, the opposite also occurs;

that is where a pleasurable thought is so intense that, again, it causes imbalance. I will give you an example. Let's say that someone says that he's very happy, because his girl-friend is beautiful, sweet-natured, intelligent. This idea dominates him, he wants to be with her and believes that he will shortly marry her. But various circumstances do not lead to marriage, the couple breaks up, and the man is overwhelmed by unhappiness, which is, of course, the opposite of the previous condition, of happiness. What should he have done to avoid all this happening? He should have accepted, of course, the pleasing relationship which he had and should have thought about his probable marriage, but he shouldn't have let his thoughts dominate him. He should have reflected that just as it was likely that he would marry the girl, it was equally likely that he wouldn't. Because nothing is certain until it has taken place. If this man had looked with the same calmness upon both possibilities, he would not have been carried away either by the one or the other."

I have to say that I didn't like this analysis, even though I saw that it was right. It seemed to me that the Master meant that happiness and unhappiness are the same thing, and I, of course, had a need for happiness, just like all of us. I voiced my objections and, moreover, quite strongly, because this was a matter which hurt me personally. I didn't want to part with the small enjoyments, whatever gave me happiness, as I believed that I would have to do.

"I didn't say that you should deprive yourself of anything", the Master replied. "On the contrary, I say that the disciple should live and enjoy everything. But what I did say was that he should not be attached to anything, because, those things which he may want are neither certain nor everlasting. Everything changes. There is another state of consciousness over and beyond happiness, which is unimpaired, which is not affected by external events and situations. It is in this that you are being trained."

"And what, in the end, is this state?"

"It is the result of absolute acceptance both of the positive and of the negative, and, naturally, of the constant balancing of them. It is then that the profound calm comes in which the mind is not affected by opposing ideas, so that it remains always at peace."

We had similar conversations again over the years, because true peace of the mind does not come easily or quickly. During this period, I observed the Master; whatever happened, he did not seem to be troubled. Although he would speak dynamically, although he frequently used unexpected ways to make us understand some difficult concept, nevertheless, behind all this, his stability, calmness, his absolute serenity were apparent. And when some disciple brought a current which concealed a one-sided approach to something, he would put forward the opposite so that balance would be recovered. If the disciple said, for example, that something which had happened to him was marvellous, that now his life would change, and so on, the Master would tell him that, of course, what had happened was very good, but that he himself would have to work in order to maintain it. Thus the enthusiasm would wane, to be replaced by alertness and activation. If, again, the opposite happened and a disciple told people that someone was a lost cause and that nothing would make him change, the Master would respond that nothing is lost and everything is possible. These words, of course, reduced the disillusionment and gave encouragement to the disciple.

All the disciples with the Master work to acquire serenity, the profound calmness of the mind, by constantly balancing the opposing forces of life. Progression continues with our life itself as our guide and with the support of the Master, who shows us the way to the final goal: union with spirituality.

DYNAMIC FUNCTIONING

My first true outburst against the Master came a few months after I met him. I remember at that time, as there had been an increase in the number of members of the Society, we decided to structure a new organised system for the groups of lessons. For that purpose, all of us older disciples met together to discuss the programme, the responsibilities each of us would have, and the way in which lessons would be conducted. Because two people were still missing, until they arrived the Master turned the discussion to the subject of narcotics, which at that time, ten years ago, was, as we all know, a very acute problem.

To begin with, the conversation proceeded calmly. We all expressed our view, pointing out the critical nature of the problem and how necessary it was for a radical solution to be found. Much was heard about the irresponsibility of drug-dealers, who invade schools in whatever way they are able and sell death to children with the sole aim of making money. Some of the disciples who had come into contact with drug-addicts described in grim colours their wretchedness and the misery of their families. The conversation had begun to become animated and we all expressed the view that these drug-sellers should be severely punished, should go to prison for life, that their profits should be confiscated, etc.

At this point, the Master intervened and said that every state should be unhesitating in imposing the death penalty on sellers of narcotics. Only in this way would this evil be combated and the needless loss of young people be stopped.

I froze. I gazed at him as if I'd been turned to stone. What was he saying? Who has the right to take away the life of another? Was this the teaching of love, then? My brain was in turmoil. From being frozen, I suddenly began to feel hot, to boil over. I was flooded with rage and anger. I broke out in words which nothing could stop.

"Come on now, Master! Nobody is God, nobody can punish with death. What are we, beasts of the jungle? Are we to be ruled by hate? Don't you always tell us to love what is evil? What you've just said is terrible, unacceptable. If you don't take it back, I'm walking out."

But does a Master ever change? He began to explain to me that I hadn't yet understood certain things, and that was why I was reacting as I did. That the death of some drug-pushers would serve as an example to others, and that only in this way would children be saved. He said that the taking of a few lives was not such a terrible thing compared with the wrongful death of so many other people. He than added the most incredible thing of all: that what he was saying was not an expression of hate, but, on the contrary, of love, a dynamic love which breaks down what is negative, even by death, if it can't happen in any other way.

At these last words of his, my cup flowed over, I got up, snatched my handbag, and walked out of the room, shouting: "I'm not having that; that's not a position a Master should take. I'm leaving." On the stairs, a disciple, who had hurried out after me, caught up with me. He tried to calm me, but I didn't listen to him. I went home in a state of rage, and this lasted for many hours.

The next day I went to the Society again, because I had an appointment with a new member. I asked a woman disciple what had happened the day before with the discussion about the programme of lessons, and she replied: "What discussion? After the position you took up, we weren't able to discuss anything else". I felt a bit bad at having caused such a hold-up in the organisation of our work, but I continued to maintain the same stance on the matter of the death penalty. This was not, in any case, strange, because I had concerned myself with this issue from an early age. I'd thought about it a lot, and had arrived at my absolute conclusions. How could I change – just because a Master professed something different?

In spite of this, and because my impressions of the teaching had so far been very favourable, I went to talk to him again. He welcomed me as though nothing had happened on the previous day, and it was I who first brought up the burning issue. The Master gave me the following analysis of his attitude:

"The Master does not wish to condemn anyone to death; he never says anything of the kind about any person or persons; because his task is the dissolution of negative situations, the factors, that is, which are personified through certain people. In the case of drug-dealers, these have been literally possessed by a mania for money, to such an extent that they are indifferent to the devastation which they are spreading. It is the mania and the passion that the Master dissolves, and not the people. If, for this to happen, it is necessary for certain people to be put to death, the sacrifice must be made, if no other measure brings results. The dissolution of passion is an expression of love, you must understand, and not of hate. Of love which necessarily uses harsh measures, if that is necessary. This resolution is a force which springs from the heart and not from some personal need or desire. Naturally, I would wish a death sentence to be the last resort, and for it to be avoided if possible. If, however, it isn't possible, then we must accept it and support it. Otherwise the mania of the drug-dealers will be strengthened and we shall lose control of them. And what interests the Master is that good should always have the upper hand."

At these words I had begun to calm down, but not completely. Love which resolves with so much force still alarmed me. I preferred the other kind of love, that which protects, as in the story of the saint who hid his brother's murderer, and this act dissolved the latter's criminal tendencies. I began, of course, to see that changes can't always be brought about by means of loving kindness and that taking a hard line is also necessary. But for me to accept equally both manifestations of love – dynamic resolution and the soul's embrace – took at least five years from the time of this episode. In the meantime, the Master sometimes used the one aspect and sometimes the other, depending upon the circumstances. And, naturally, the disciples reacted accordingly; they wanted the motherly acceptance, but turned away from the fatherly anger of the Master.

Those who meet the Master for the first time are impressed by the power which they see in his words, in his look, in his patience, and in the healings of the sick which he performs. I often hear someone who is ill say that his body is flooded with power when the Master is giving him therapy.

In order for us to be trained in dynamic functioning we have received many varied lessons. One of these has been regular daily exercise of certain physical movements. The movements have as their aim to bring down to earth, first, the power within the body and then to spread it in space. During the first six months of my discipleship I did these exercises every morning, and then sat down to meditate. I always noticed a change in my physical body, as well as in the disposition of the soul. I overflowed with a current of energy, which helped me in whatever I wanted to do for many hours.

To begin with, I didn't much believe that certain movements are capable of empowering man. I knew, of course, that in the atmosphere there are many and various currents of energy which affect man, but I hadn't imagined that it was ever possible for someone to direct them at will. And yet this is what happens with the exercises: man learns to handle the powers rather than being their servant. By regular work, I felt that I was taking into my hands the energies which encircled me, I was bringing them into the body, which was revitalised immediately. Later, I was able to take them wherever I wanted, to perform therapy, to spread them from the heart, and to keep them in my body, for it to be strong. And I learnt that when this vehicle takes on strength, man can through special exercises also break down the negative forces which are diffused in space.

All this process lasted as long as was needed to bring the result: that is, an absolute awareness of the capability of man of being the handler of energies and powers. Now I don't need such work. Quite simply, every moment when I reflect that I am filled with power, this happens instantaneously, and, naturally, the power which I experience I diffuse again instantaneously wherever I wish, wherever there is weakness and illness. Some members ask me if I'm tired by what I do, whether the discussions with people and the healings exhaust me. When I say that I'm not tired, they don't greatly believe me, and I have to explain that I've learnt how to renew myself rapidly whenever I have transferred power from my body to others. This, of course, happens automatically, without thinking, just as breathing happens. Why should we feel ourselves to be weak when around us there is an unlimited power which passes through us constantly and regenerates our existence?

As I began to gain strength through exercise, by an understanding of human possibilities, and the practice of spiritual healing, the Master set me certain tasks for the Society. But I noticed that I often lost the power as I attempted to put this into practice. It was as if something was making me withdraw within myself, so that I didn't dare to express myself, and became imprisoned by an undefined weakness.

One of the most typical events of that period had to do with the efforts which I made to find a photograph showing the rising of the sun. This was going to be enlarged and hung up at the Society. I looked everywhere I could for a picture of sunrise, in books, in photography, in shops selling slides. Whatever I found wasn't what we wanted; it didn't satisfy me at all. One day I thought I'd found the right photograph and asked for it to be enlarged. But this so distorted the sun that it was no longer recognisable as the sun. I took the enlarged photograph and showed it to the Master, although I knew that I ought to have torn it up. His reaction was so unexpected that I was rendered speechless. He shouted for at least ten minutes, so violently that I didn't have chance to utter a word. He said that it was completely wrong for me to show the Master such a warped photograph and not do on my own what I had to do with it.

I left him like a lost soul, without understanding what finally had happened. Of course, I regarded his attitude to such a simple matter as exaggerated. Some time had to pass before I realised that he was not concerned about the photograph not being a success, but about my own stance. I had wanted yet again to drop the problem and the failure on the Master, and not to sort it out myself. But such an attitude is that of an immature child and not of a dynamic, spiritual person. Power – I came to understand over the years – shows itself everywhere alike and not only at certain moments in life. And since at that time I had begun to be aware of the existence of this power, I had to start to express it in all my jobs, in every instance, and without inhibitions. You can't be a spiritual healer – which means a channel of pure power to the person who is ill – if you are not at the same time a responsible person, if you don't stand on your own feet in any work which you have to see through, even in some conversation which you will have.

One day I happened to be present when a disciple came to tell the Master what he had done over some particular matter. He spoke dynamically, he described the events in a lively manner, he showed great decisiveness in his words. I admired his power and I would very much have liked to be like him. When he left and I was left alone for a little while with the Master, I expressed my admiration for the dynamic functioning of the disciple. He surprised me by the answer which he gave: "No, Mrs Klairi," he said, "this attitude isn't power, it doesn't stem from the real inner nature, the entity. On the contrary, it stems from his need to appear important, to dominate others, to satisfy his egoism. What he said and did was the result of weakness and not of power. Because true power is something else, it doesn't come from the needs of the personality, but only from the deeper consciousness, which doesn't have needs; it's complete, autonomous, and simply manifests itself dynamically in whatever way it must. How could power be something which comes from a self-centred need? It is weakness, in spite of the fact that it seems like strength."

This reply satisfied me completely, because I realised how often human appearances are misinterpreted and lure us into false conclusions. What, however, I didn't understand was why the Master didn't tell the disciple that his attitude was coming from weakness, but allowed him to think the opposite, while at other times he functioned by breaking down such manifestations directly. To this doubt I received the answer that the approach of a Master is differentiated according to the case. When someone is ready to accept the fact that he is weak, then he speaks to him about his weakness, but when he can't bear to find out where in reality he is, then he leaves him for a while, or at certain moments only, to function as he wishes. In watching his disciples closely, the Master 'plays', I would say, with the energies and powers, leading them by various pathways to a rising up of the inner self.

I looked at the Master in surprise. Suddenly a concept which was completely new had entered into me. The concept of true dynamic functioning. Power doesn't mean only dissolution, it doesn't mean shouting - or necessarily new directions. It means, as well, incredible patience, the maintaining of certain situations for as long as they are needed, tolerance, and a profound understanding of human needs. Dynamic functioning is at one and the same time a smile, a caress, a telling-off, a conversation, or a ban. But where is this power, which takes on so many forms, springing from?

I began to meditate on the subject of 'power' very regularly and I received certain answers. These satisfied me up to a point, but they didn't show me what its source is. I looked at its manifestations with different symbols, I did mental analyses of superficial power, which is generated by human weaknesses, but the crucial question was not answered satisfactorily.

One day, when I was in a state of complete calm, when I didn't want anything and no problem was bothering me, I became submerged within myself again, without thinking what I wanted to meditate on. At that moment, an enchanting vision unfolded before me, completely of its own accord, and I saw it from behind my closed eyelids as clearly as if I were watching a film in colour. Through a circle which was completely empty, colourless – a circle of non-existence, you might say – multi-coloured radiations, which moved like rotating undulations, were springing forth. These radiations had tremendous power, and wherever they ended up, they created forms: bodies of human beings, of animals, of plants. As their movement towards the forms continued, these dissolved and others took their place. The same thing happened ceaselessly, and I, in wonder, watched, absorbing everything into myself. And there came a moment when I realised that I had been so carried away by the spectacle that I had forgotten that empty circle, the source of all the forces. I looked again carefully and saw that the circle was always the same, absolutely void and colourless, while around it a world was being created and re-created constantly.

When the meditation finished, I began to think about its meaning. It wasn't difficult to link it with the subject that was on my mind at that time: what is the source of this power with its many forms. It was perfectly obvious that its source was nothing, the completely empty field of the circle. But why was this revelation given to me on that specific day, when I'd not looked for it, and why hadn't it been given to me all the time that I was searching for it? Then I remembered the state I was in before I meditated, the state of completeness which does not want anything. I was, that is to say, myself void, empty at that time - and yet full, because there was no need within me. And what I was projected as an empty circle. But this is the sole source of power, it is the state of non-desire!

Amazing, superb! You don't want anything and then you become all the powers of life! You handle them only in order to create, to mould and remould, to spread beauty, completeness, to imbue every situation. 'My Master, my self, diffuse consciousness', I said then to the higher entity which gives us everything, 'how incomprehensible and indescribable you are! How much I want never to forget your presence!'

I got up from where I was and the room around me seemed changed. Everything was different. Everything was so beautiful, so simple! This state of well-being lasted for some hours, but in the days which followed, I frequently brought it back within myself. However, it did not come to me to be able to remain permanently in that state. Personal needs sprang up every so often and interrupted the dynamic functioning which I had experienced when I was meditating. Needs which distracted me with a thousand 'I wants', and I would forget that whenever we want something, we are not complete, and so we are not really strong. Stability in a state of completeness comes through the years, with much patience, and with great will for its realisation, which is deliverance from the bonds of desires and the uninterrupted manifestation of power and love.

DISCIPLE - MASTER RELATIONS

One of the greatest problems in discipleship is the relations between the Master and the disciple, or, to express it rather better, the ideas of the disciple about the form of their relations. I became aware of this problem only after five or six years as a disciple, in spite of the fact that the Master pointed it out to us very frequently, so that we could see it and overcome it. The specific problem is one of dependence and a continuation of all the previous problems of man, which are due to attraction and repulsion, the two great powers of life.

The Master, in speaking on this topic, says that as long as the disciple maintains an 'astral' relation with his

Master, he cannot go on to substantive spiritual union with him. But what does 'astral' mean? This word was heard quite often at the Society when I first went there, particularly among the disciples. The way in which it was said indicated a contempt for, a rejection of whatever was astral. You heard them, for example, talking scornfully about astral meditations, about an astral approach, astral relations, and so on. I suspected at that time that the 'astral' is connected with certain weaknesses, desires, imaginings, but its meaning wasn't too clear to me.

It isn't possible at the moment for me to enter, in this book, into an extensive analysis of the astral, which is a vast field of consciousness, with many fields and subfields. I shall say only a few words in order to show what are the astral relations which the disciple wishes to have with the Master. 'Astral' is that state of man in which there are many unsatisfied desires, that is, desires which have not been fulfilled, and, therefore, resolved. The 'unsatisfied' in man is the totality of his desires, which, when these can't be satisfied by himself, seek their satisfaction by some other person or thing. For as long as this satisfaction does not come, the desire grows and often leads the individual to daydreams and fantasies. A very common example of this state is the emotionalism of an adolescent who wants to make love for the first time. His desire for sex is personified in a person, and the fantasies about that person begin. When the sexual act takes place, the fantasies cease – if, of course, he is a normal person – because the desire has been fulfilled.

But let's see what happens with disciples, who, as human beings, also have many unsatisfied desires and seek from someone or something to fulfil them. When they get to know the Master, they personify their needs in his person and they imagine him giving them everything they want. Some are seeking a father, others a friend, others a protector. But these are ideas which do not correspond to reality, to the pure spiritual relations which Masters teach to their disciples, relations which they must have, in any event, with the whole of life. Until spirituality is developed, disciples are under astral influence, that is, they are governed by their unsatisfied desires and imagine that the Master will fulfil them.

One thing which surprised me enormously in the early stages were the questions which some people asked about the Master: "How old is the Master?" somebody asked. "Forty", I said. "Ah! Is that all?" he replied, and a look of disappointment was imprinted on his face. Because he didn't want the Master to be young. The reality didn't correspond to his desire. He felt a repulsion from his age, because his model of a Master was for him identified with an old man, a revered elder.

Somebody else asked: "What education has the Master had?" "Education isn't necessary for someone to be a

Master", I replied. And this person looked at me as if he didn't believe me, as if I had demolished some fine vision for him and he no longer knew what to rely upon. Another very disappointing answer which I had to give was that the Master is Greek. "Oh, so he's not a foreigner?" I would be asked again distrustfully. "No, he's an Athenian, born in Peristeri", I would say, laughing secretly inside myself when I later realised how much importance some still attached to the district in which a Master was born. And sometimes it amused me to add the last reply, which would break down anything astral. "The Master", I would say, "is married with two children". "Really?" some would say. "Fancy that!" was the response of others, and their eyes would open wide.

Fortunately, when I met the Master, I had no idea what a Master meant, and so there wasn't anything that I was expecting from him. Of course, I had imagined him as an old ascetic – perhaps I was influenced by antiquity and religion – but after the first surprise and some fleeting doubts, I stopped being concerned with his age and the fact that he was married. But later, as my unsatisfied desires and needs came to light, I too began to personify him as I wished at the time. And, of course, this made my learning experience difficult, because the Master teaches the disciple to find completeness within himself and not in the person of someone else.

One of the most striking instances which show how disappointed a disciple can be by the Master when the latter is not as he has imagined him occurred in the second month of my discipleship. Striking – and comical, I would say. At that time the Master was showing us how we must learn to play different roles, to become actors, mimics, to unite ourselves, that is, with all aspects of mankind.

Of this teaching and its importance I shall speak, with details, in the next book. That day, at a time when the group included many young people, some of them had bought packets of potato crisps and were eating them as they listened to the Master. He took a packet which was offered to him and ate a crisp now and again as he jokingly played various roles. The next day, a very young girl told us that she was leaving the Society. When I asked her why, she replied that it was unthinkable for her to accept as a Master someone who ate crisps!

Although this occurrence demonstrates the girl's immaturity, I mention it to show the peculiarities which develop in the relation of the disciple to the Master. If a few crisps which the Master ate occasionally were enough to drive someone away from the teaching, it goes without saying that many stronger needs affect the relationship of disciples with Masters. Needs deeply rooted within them by the experiences and deprivations of the whole of life.

But what is it that the disciple really wants and thinks that he wants? Why are these two wills often opposed, even though the person does not realise it himself? Deep down, everybody seeks after freedom, autonomy, and the development of his consciousness. There is, however, also his childishness, which constantly seeks to receive, to be protected, to be satisfied. This childishness conflicts continually with the need for maturity, and since every Master always teaches maturity, major inner tensions and problems are created in disciples.

Once the Master said that whereas the disciple comes to solve his problems, the Master brings him new problems, greater obstacles and trials. "That's just what I needed", I thought at the time. "As if I didn't have enough problems, so I am going to have more added?" I didn't speak, of course, I didn't express my thoughts, but I soon realised that I was not going to escape from him easily. "The Master – my problem", I began to call him inside myself. Naturally, the problem lies elsewhere; it lies in the weaknesses of the disciple, who is tested every so often in expressing power and overcoming all the obstacles of his personality.

In order to understand the issue of the obstacles which are put up by a Master, we began to read and to study carefully the labours of Hercules. In these can be seen all the trials which Eurystheus set for him to become a hero. That was all very well, and certainly they demonstrate that man progresses by way of obstacles, because in this way he is strengthened and develops, but how is he to endure until such development comes, and he becomes a hero-Hercules?

As we disciples progressed step by step to finding our true self, we saw how difficult it was to leave behind the old way of life, to abandon those habits which keep the individual in immaturity. And very often, when we were not successful, we shifted the blame on to the Master. I can remember once when the Master had urged me to stop being so concerned with myself and to begin to help those who needed it, I was very upset. I made efforts, I meditated on the matter, I tried not to think of my own individual problems. I didn't manage it, however, and new personal needs came to dominate me.

So then I took my pen and wrote in my file: "I want to serve, I want to help others, but I am not up to it. I feel that I am being lost and don't exist. And I still need my old familiar self. What is going to happen to that, is it going to disappear?" And the more I resisted the inclination of my soul to learn to love people, the more difficult things became. And in order to justify my attitude, I let doubts flood my brain: "How do I know", I asked myself, "whether the direction the Master takes is the right one? It would be a good idea for me to leave him for a while. How can I be sure that he's teaching us what is good and right?" In this way I transposed my own problem on to him, in an effort to rid myself of my guilt feelings.

How often have I heard disciples complaining to the Master about some job which they thought was too difficult! And how often have they loaded their errors and failures on to him, saying that he shouldn't have set them such a task. And he would answer, somewhat ironically: "Ah yes! Of course, blame it on the Master". Some years have to pass for it to be realised that blame lies in the weakness of the disciple and that the problem is within him and not in the wider consciousness which guides him to gain strength. Because it is not easily understood that the task of the Master is the raising of the consciousness. Disciples are looking for other things from him, depending upon their development in each case, and this is the reason why they react unfavourably to the awakening of the higher self, the pure spiritual being which seeks to be expressed by everyone.

One day when I had been seized by despair over my difficulties, I said to the Master: "What's going to become of me? I'm filled with fears, rages, doubts. I don't think I'm any good as a disciple when I'm weak like this. I feel that my thoughts are ridiculous and my brain is stupid. How am I to make any progress?" I was asking him in despair to support me, because I had become completely disillusioned. At such moments the Master responds by taking the burden from the disciple, since he sees that the disciple is not equal to it. So he said to me: "I think that you are doing very well. Little by little you are learning to dominate your weaknesses and that is what matters. All in good time. You will wake up one day and you'll see that you have changed. And then all your life will change. But I'm pleased with you."

How much I liked his attitude, because that's the way I wanted the Master: calm, soft, taking our problems from us and not constantly giving us new ones. Why does he pressure us so much? Why does he push us all the time towards new achievements? Aren't we alright as we are?

Of course we're not alright! Who can be alright when he's governed by a thousand and one difficulties and obsessions? I remember how hard the Master worked to rid me of one such fixation. Ever since I was a little girl I had had a great distaste for having anything to do with financial matters. I didn't want to handle money at all. I was very pleased that my father and later my husband took all the responsibilities for the economic needs of the family. I worked, of course, I earned a salary, but I always put it into the common fund in order to be rid of the troublesome presence of money. It felt very good for me to take back what I needed for the expenses of the house, as long as I didn't have the responsibility for safekeeping of the money and for the bills. My refusal also extended to whatever else had to do with financial matters. I hated commerce, I avoided accounting, I never went to the tax office.

I learnt through my discipleship that every repulsion conceals a corresponding attraction. In studying my unjustifiable attitude towards money, I very soon discovered that I didn't want to handle it because I was afraid of losing it. I didn't want to have the obligation to give money to anybody, and since I never had on me more than a very little, I couldn't give anything. And I didn't want to give, not only so that I shouldn't be deprived myself, but also because I was afraid that other people would exploit me. And I couldn't stand that.

Through this problem, which I had buried within myself for years, very soon burst out and began to cause reactions in me. The first of these was over the decision that we took that all the members should pay a subscription for the upkeep of the Society. It took me time to accept even such a simple and completely reasonable thing and to share without difficulty in the common expenses. To realise, that is, that the decision of the management council of the Society, of which, anyway, I was the secretary, was not asking for anything strange, nor was it exploiting anybody.

Since the money issue had taken on very large dimensions in my mind, the Master entrusted me with making purchases of the things which the Society needed. I didn't like this responsibility at all, not because I would be spending money – the purchases were made from the Society's common funds – but because at that time I was excessively afraid of failure. What would happen if I spent money which wasn't mine and the things I chose were ugly or unsuitable? I went, of course, to buy what I had to, but I always tried to have another member with me, to share the responsibilities with him.

Everything which had to do with the money issue and what I learnt about it always brought to mind what I had learnt from numerology about the number twelve. Twelve symbolises the trials through which man goes as he begins to work on offering service to others. In the book of the Tarot there is a representation of these trials on one of its cards. This shows the disciple, that is, the person being tested, hanging upside-down from a branch of a tree to which his left foot is tied. His head and his hands are pointing downwards, and gold coins are falling from his pockets. The coins symbolise knowledge, which the disciple being tested decides to give to people, the wealth of inner values. So when I was asked to use money for the work, the image from the Tarot came immediately to my mind and tormented me. Because I had absolutely no desire to be hung up by the feet like that, even if this was simply a symbol.

The Master in various ways showed me my error over the money issue. Even by his own attitude he taught me what I should do. I'd seen him give whatever he had or didn't have to people who had economic problems. And this was particularly significant because the Master was never a rich man. However, my own difficulty could in no way be overcome.

One day, when I still continued to take the same attitude towards money, he asked me to take all the banknotes out off my purse. Then, when we'd counted them, I waited uncomfortably to see what he would do. I was thinking that although it wasn't all that much money, nevertheless I cared about what its fate could be. Then the Master in a grave manner told me to put all the notes in an ashtray and asked me, holding a lighted match in his hand: "What would you say if I proposed that we should burn them?" I looked at him thunder-struck. We should burn the money? But why? Wouldn't it be a sin? Wouldn't it be better for us to buy something with it so it shouldn't be wasted? But he replied that if we burnt it, it would be as if we were burning my bonds with it, as if we were breaking down the astral relation I had with it.

I began to wonder what this mad idea was now. Why didn't he ever leave me in peace? And why, after all, should I agree with him? I'm under absolutely no obligation to accept what he says, and particularly when that isn't rationally explicable and is unacceptable. But as I was thinking, I saw that in the end I had to pass the test, because in that way I would probably be rescued from a major obstacle of a whole lifetime. The first match burnt out, a second was lit, a third, and finally I agreed that the money should be burnt, and, moreover, without any resistance, but with complete calm. Then the Master took me by surprise again by saying that I could put the money back in my purse, because his aim was not that the money should be burnt, but that the astral relation which I had with it, as he'd explained to me previously, should be burnt.

This event helped me to accept another manifestation of the Master, at the time when I regarded him as my biggest problem. Of course, I was not delivered at once from the fixation I had with money which had tormented me for years. A long time passed before a more substantive change took place, and I went through various financial situations before changing attitude. But then a beginning had been made. Today I handle the funds of the Society, of the family, and of the publishing house which we have founded. I go to the bank and to the tax office, and I keep the accounts, when necessary, without any problem. For a period, moreover, I had the management of a ceramic jewellery enterprise which we set up, together with other disciples, to support the work of the Society financially. The substantive change which took place within me thanks to these experiences was that I stopped shifting the responsibilities for money matters on to the Master, saying that he was to blame whenever any difficulty made its appearance.

"The disciple", says the Master, "is being trained to become a handler of energies and powers. Money is itself a form of energy. He has, therefore, to learn to handle it, to increase it, to use it where it should be used, generally to utilise it correctly and coolly. Only in this way can he meet his own needs and those of his family, and support financially the work he wishes to do for others. Every form of energy must be his tool and not his master."

The teaching of synthesis covers all areas of life. It teaches autonomy everywhere, in everything. At the beginning, this is the disciple's great problem, because he is afraid to become autonomous. He seeks from the Master a substitute for what he lacks. In the early months of my learning process, I saw the Master behaving like a father to the younger disciples, discussing with them even the simplest things – how long they slept, what they ate, if they went for walks, and so on. Later, he left them more free to decide on such matters. This change made some of them react unfavourably; they thought that his interest had diminished, now he was caring more for other people, in other words, they couldn't stand losing a good daddy and were jealous of the others who seemed to be taking their place, as is the case with younger siblings in a family.

Much later, and when I had now started to appreciate the significance of dynamic functioning and the spiritual relationship which must develop between the disciple and Master, he put me to a new test. He told me, at a time which was totally inappropriate because of various circumstances and changes in the structure of the Society, that I must very soon find another building, to open another Society. I replied immediately: "That can't happen now, Master; it's not the right moment". I saw that the disciples who were with us wore a lost expression and seemed to be waiting for a telling-off from the Master for my refusal. But he said: "I'm very glad about your attitude. It shows maturity and correct relationship with the Master". It is obvious from these words that the chief concern of the Master is the firm establishment of the disciple in a position of autonomy and much less the expression of some task. What is important is that any work, even the refusal to carry it out, should spring from inner power and not from a dependence which forces the disciple to obey, because he's afraid to say what he believes and what he wants to do.

In essence, there is no problem for disciples with regard to a specific Master. The disciples only see it that way because they are unable or don't want to see where their problem lies. However, this always relates to their consciousness, to the inner Master. It is to him that they are putting up resistance and opposition, transforming him into some person. As the years pass, as the concept of inner awareness develops and is put into action, the relations of disciples with Masters change and a completely different flow shows itself towards the task, which is a joint one for the development of spirituality and its spread to a great many people.

RESISTANCES OF THE PERSONALITY

"Mrs Klairi, the time has come for you to go and pay a visit to your old friends. You've been in the Society for eight months now, and you haven't told them what you're doing and what you've been busy with all this time."

It was with these words that the Master greeted me one day, and I had the shock of my life. I never imagined that my relations with my old acquaintances were of any importance for my discipleship. So I asked him immediately why there had to be such a resumption of connections. His reply was:

"Because your attitude to these ladies isn't at all right. You've suddenly stopped communicating with them, and you've left them without any explanation. But in this way you're provoking them to think ill of you, and that's a mistake."

"And what's it matter to me what they think? That's their problem, not mine."

"No, it's yours as well, because you're the cause of it, with the attitude you take. And you take it because you don't come clean with yourself."

"What do you mean, I don't come clean with myself? I don't understand."

"Quite simply, you are avoiding having this meeting because you don't yet dare to tell anybody anything about the discipleship you're following. Just think: you are being taught the truth, and you hide this fact from others. It's a mistake, and shows weakness and doubts about the teaching you are receiving."

"But I talk about everything to many people, Master."

"Others are not the same thing as the people you used to know. To these you should give an explanation, because you owe it to them. In any case, don't forget their support in the past."

"But I haven't a clue whether they're interested in the teaching. So why should I talk to them about what I'm taught?"

"It shouldn't concern you how they will react. The individual must have the courage to show what he is; how much more so when this is his work for spirituality. Others may have their own views, which are all to be respected."

"You're right, Master, but as this issue has arisen very suddenly for me, I want to think about it for a few days."

We agreed that I should wait a little, until I was ready for the meeting, and I began to think about the matter. But because I really had a difficulty in doing what I should, the Master launched a second attack.

"What's happening, Mrs Klairi, to what we said about the visit to your friends?"

"What shall I say, Master? It seems ridiculous to me suddenly now to gather them all together and begin to talk to them. It's all very artificial, this affair. I don't like it."

"There's no need for you to see them all together. Go to the house of one of the ladies, whichever you like, and it's the same thing."

"And what am I to say to her? Something doesn't feel right here."

"It doesn't feel right for the reasons I've told you. But it's very simple. You'll explain what it is you've been doing all this time; you'll explain, with all the truth, why you've withdrawn from them, and, naturally, you'll ask them to forgive you for your unjustifiable attitude, your silence, and your distance."

"Ah, I see. Now I'll ask for pardon as though I've committed some sin...".

"The sin is your inner resistance, a refusal to communicate with some people. So then, what's going to happen, when are you going to go to your friend's?"

At that moment a disciple came to discuss something urgent with the Master and I slipped away from him, in order to escape from an unwelcome conversation. And on the days which followed I avoided seeing him on my own, in case he started up again with the same subject. Until the third attack came, and this was abrupt and absolute.

"So. Tomorrow morning, you'll make a phone call and you'll make a date with your friend. This affair has gone on long enough."

"But...".

"There are no 'buts'. You have got to get through this field, and you are well aware of the reasons. Let's not talk about it any more."

So that was it... An end to the postponements. So how are you going to talk now to somebody, somebody you are very fond of, of course, about things so different from her own ideas. But I now knew very well that I wouldn't escape from this bitter cup. I telephoned my friend, she was very glad to hear from me, and we fixed a meeting for two days later. I would go to her house, which was in a northern suburb.

The fateful day came. I got up with a heavy heart and went to open the window. What a surprise – and what joy!... The streets were white over; it had snowed during the night. Great! I couldn't go to the suburb under snow. I telephoned the Master in triumph: "I can't go!" "Why?" "There's snow on the ground; my friend lives outside Athens." "Then you'll put snow-chains on your car and go." "I don't have snow-chains." "Then buy some, Mrs Klairi. We mustn't let resistances of the personality defeat us. Not to say that you have caused the snow by your attitude." "Sorry, what was that you said?" "Nothing, nothing, we'll talk about it in the evening – when you get back from your friend's." And the telephone went dead.

So, snow-chains it would have to be. A perilous journey. I kept losing my way, and finding it again, until at last I arrived. And there were the astonished eyes of my friend when she saw me arriving up to the knees in snow. She hadn't expected me in such weather.

The conversation began, after the embraces and the kisses, and everything went... appallingly! I had never in my life had a more insipid conversation. I said, of course, everything that I should have said, but how did I say it. I didn't deliver any message, either about the issue of the Society, or my attitude towards it, or about the forgiveness I was seeking. I left with the impression that my friend had not understood why I had visited her. It was as if what I said didn't have the power to come across to her.

And then I went to the Society. As soon as the Master saw me, he said: "You haven't passed through the field,

Mrs Klairi. You haven't shown what you are doing, you haven't expressed any power, nor have you united yourself in soul with your friend." Naturally, although I told him everything that I had said, I knew that he was right. In any event, my expression showed that I had failed, that in essence I hadn't dared to speak with assurance about the spiritual work, about the changes which were taking place within me, the teaching I was receiving. The Master then said that we would leave the matter for a short while, but I was to bear in mind that it wasn't closed and that later I would have to make a second contact.

I calmed down a little, and stayed with him without speaking. I knew that he was right about everything and there was no need for me to say any more. Then he reminded me of what he'd said to me on the telephone: that I had caused the snow. This remark again aroused my interest, and I asked him to explain what he meant.

"It's simple. Your reaction to the visit was so extreme, your thoughts were so negative, that these brought about the abrupt change in the weather and the sudden snow."

"But how is it possible for the attitude of one person to affect the weather conditions? I can't believe that sort of thing. I don't understand how there can be so much power inside me."

"Are you forgetting, Mrs Klairi, what used to happen in the past, before you met the Master? You yourself said at one time that you were always ill-wishing people, that all it needed was for you to look at somebody or something, and a disaster would occur. So why to you find this so strange now?"

"But it's one thing to ill-wish a person and another to ill-wish, so to speak, the weather."

"There isn't as much difference as you think, because it isn't so much the range of the thing which is affected by some current which matters as the force which passes through it. If this is great, then the energy is transferred dynamically and produces changes, positive or negative, depending upon the quality of the thought and the origination."

"But I told you before that I don't feel that I have so much power that I can cause snow. In any case, I had had absolutely no thought, my mind had not gone in the slightest to the idea of snow. So how can you say that I caused it?"

"You didn't have any such thought, that's certain. But you had some other thoughts – that you didn't want to go to your friend's house. Of course, you'd decided to go, but deep down you didn't want to. Your refusal worked in your unconscious, and, because it was very powerful, magnetised an obstacle to come so that you could escape the visit. The obstacle came through the snow."

"So, in the end, is the unconscious so powerful? I can't believe that somebody, without realising anything, without being aware of what is happening within him, can emit such forces. It seems to me really inexplicable, improbable."

"And yet, before you met me, a lot happened. You yourself have told me that once you looked at a baby's pram, and immediately the four wheels fell off. Another time you thought something about a person and he fell down, vomited, and so on. How do you explain these things?"

"As you said, Master. My thought concealed something negative, even if I didn't know it – it was totally unconscious – and the negative origination caused the occurrence. When, for example, I admired the beautiful pram, I suppose that unconsciously I would have liked my own children to have one like it. And so, although there was admiration, there was also envy, which was more powerful than the admiration and damaged the pram. But that was one thing, when it was a personal matter; the snow which affected a whole city was another. I mean, I can understand that the negative unconscious wish of an individual can affect another individual, or even an object. Because here there is a certain quantitative balance, that is, it's a case of two people who have equal forces to some extent. And so one of them emits his force to the other, who, since he's not stronger, succumbs to this force and is affected. But I don't see how an individual force – mine in the present instance – can defeat the collective force by causing changes in the weather. Because the weather didn't only affect me; it affected all the residents of Athens. That's why I can't accept that I caused the snow."

"You are seeing the issue in a limited manner, and that's why you don't understand it. You speak about your own unconscious and don't acknowledge that it is a part of the common, the group unconscious, which is expressed by all human beings. Every negative thought stems from the resistance of the individual ego, that is, of the limited human consciousness. But the limited consciousness is not only individual, just as, anyway, no idea, force, energy, and so on is individual. We have said that all these things are fields within the Entity. Since, therefore, every negative idea is expressed in the ontological field, it is externalised by all those people who become its channels. And they become its channels because, for reasons which have to do with their disposition of soul, they don't become channels of the opposite thought – the positive.

"Now, as far as the specific matter of the snow goes, you became a channel for a negative idea, which is not, of course, the snow, but is the resistance of the personality. What had the Master asked of you? Why, exactly the opposite – that you should not resist union with your friends, and that you should open your self to them. Your difficulty in doing this, although it was individual, was also at the same time collective. Because many people have the same resistances, they are deluged by the same self-centred currents. So you became a receiver of the collective currents – all the time unconsciously, of course – which used you as a channel so that the obstacle – the snow – would come, which would prevent you from the expression of union. But it wasn't only a case of their using you: you also used them, you let yourself become a channel of refusal of union, without, of course, knowing it, as I said. And you allowed what happened to happen, because you didn't want to do what you had to, that is, to break down the resistances of the personality.

"But why did the obstacle present itself by means of the snow? Something had to be put forward, since you no longer dared to put forward your refusal to the Master in the open. If you had done so, if you'd gone on not listening to my advice, then another external obstacle wouldn't have been necessary. We all know that snow is a problem for traffic. And you knew it, of course, and in spite of the fact that you didn't think of it at all, the knowledge was there in your unconscious. The knowledge came, then, to bring about the sudden change in the weather. Perhaps you'll tell me that any other obstacle could have occurred; for example, your friend could have cancelled the meeting. Naturally, something else could have happened. But what happened was the most striking, the most unexpected. Because the moment had come for you to receive a big lesson about the subconscious, the diffuse consciousness brought the snow.

"We see, then, that the great unconscious also caused a major shock by the consciousness, so that you were given the lesson which you needed, so that you see the power of resistances, which are both collective and individual, as we have said. And this is why I told you on the telephone that we shall not allow the resistances of the personality to defeat us. I wasn't speaking only of your personality, but generally of the 'personality' field, which belongs to all, to the Entity.

"The disciple must express dynamically the positive aspects, in order to balance the negative. You, as an individual, didn't want to do it, and you were flooded by the collective refusal, which reached such intensity that it caused a sudden snowfall."

"I have the impression that you are telling me about two conflicting camps, the positive and the negative, and that each person expresses either the one or the other, depending on which he belongs to. That is, quite simply, his presence in one of the two strengthens it and externalises it."

"Yes, that's roughly the way it is. The opposing forces are diffused everywhere over a large range and seek channels to be given expression. Naturally, as we have said, our aim must be harmonisation and not constant conflict between them."

"But all this that you tell me is appalling. Because if humanity, unconsciously, of course, projects so many negative forces, then it's never going to evolve. Painful and destructive things are going to happen all the time."

"No, you mustn't think like that. Because, although the unconscious is vast, it isn't only negative. Often, human beings express positive forces, love, acceptance, and so on, which they don't know exist within them. And then there is all the field of which humanity has become conscious. We all know, consciously in this case, that there should be world peace, we all want humanity to have good health, not to suffer, not to be tormented by economic problems, to advance spiritually, and to develop. This, in any event, is what is being done by the churches and by spiritual people more generally. Let's not forget the collective manifestations of this, such as processions, prayers, meditations. All these things are methods of collective conscious work, carried out in order to magnetise the positive. And precisely because it is done consciously, it is capable of bringing substantive results, because people, through the disposition and will of their soul, become channels of positive forces. As consciousness expands, humanity advances increasingly into conscious functioning.

"The disciple is being trained in precisely this: to become consciously a channel of the positive. Through meditation, he reinforces and works for the good. You yourself, for example, no longer act, except in rare instances, as a channel of the negative. So everything's going well, you've changed a lot from what you were in the past."

Here the matter was dropped, as was the issue of my next contact with my friends, which was going to have to await a greater maturity – and, consequently, a reduction of the resistances – on my part. I worked on the matter of the needs and reactions of the personality continually, in order to prepare myself for that contact, but also, more generally, for all day-to-day functions. Suddenly, something totally different happened, another event, which brought the solution to the problem in a way which I didn't expect.

One day another disciple and I went to visit a certain gentleman, to perform a business transaction with him. I shall not mention here the nature of the transaction, because then I would have to speak about the work which this gentleman did, which would very probably reveal his name. I can say only that this individual was very rich and that his house possessed grandeur and stateliness.

As we entered the house, and knowing the financial standing of our host, I had a strange – and negative – impression, because the reception area was – in my opinion, of course – deplorable, it didn't fit with the house as a whole. I began to think that this probably showed a contemptuous attitude towards visitors, and the idea of this possibility annoyed me a good deal. Then, while I was racking my brain over the inappropriateness of this place, the dog of the house came up to me and bit my hand so badly that my arm was paralysed to the shoulder. Everybody hurried to help me, but the pain continued, because it seems that the dog's teeth had struck a nerve. I was in so much pain that I wasn't interested in understanding why this had happened. But later the Master explained to me that the dog's aggressiveness was caused by my own negative attitude. Not of course that the dog understood my thoughts about his master, but he had simply protected himself against my own negative current, which he had become aware of through his powerful instinct.

In pain and holding my bitten hand, a little later I went, with the other disciple, into the room where the gentleman was waiting for us. He apologised for the dog, but said it was a very rare occurrence for it to be so fierce. We then talked about the matter of the transaction which we wanted, without getting anywhere.

Since the disciple who was with me had a better grasp of the affair, I had the opportunity to look around the room we were now in. As I had not learnt my lesson from the episode with the dog, I continued to think in a negative way. I couldn't understand why the room was so overloaded, oppressive, repellent. Nor could I understand why, in this enormous house, this gentleman had accumulated in just one room, his study, his bed and a thousand and one other objects. I felt despondency mixed with contempt.

We returned to the Society disappointed by our failure in our business, and myself particularly bothered by the whole occurrence with the bite and my depressing thoughts. When the Master heard what had happened, and when he had explained to us what was going on with the dog, he spoke to me individually:

"Mrs Klairi, you must put right what you did to that gentleman. You can't behave in such a negative way towards a person, or towards a place. You must go and ask his pardon for what you thought about him."

I knew from the previous experience with my friends that it was useless to object. And anyway, the Master's analysis of my whole attitude had convinced me that the time had now come for me to control my thoughts and to direct them in a proper manner. So for that reason I immediately put into practice the Master's advice; I arranged a second meeting with the gentleman and soon went to see him. I was, of course, a little nervous, but this was not due to resistance, it was a normal state of anyone before making a spiritual opening.

What happened at this meeting left me thunderstruck, and, of course, confirmed for me the importance of a positive projection. When I went into that now familiar room, the gentleman asked me the reason why I'd asked to see him again. I replied that I wanted to ask his forgiveness, and he, naturally enough, wanted to know what he had to forgive me for. I explained to him that the last time I had had ugly thoughts about him and his house. He insisted on hearing what these thoughts were, but his manner was imbued with goodness and acceptance. I told him everything I had thought, and then he, as if he hadn't attached any importance to that, but as if he were impressed only by the whole happening, asked me to talk to him about the work of the Society.

The conversation took another turn, I spoke, I explained the aims of the Society, what we wanted to do and what had been done up to that time. The gentleman listened to me with great interest, and, moreover, at his request I enrolled him as a member of the Society at that very moment. But the most amazing thing happened a little before I left. As I was explaining to him that, in order for the work to expand, we would have to have a very large building, he said to me, very simply: "I will give you my house". I thought that I hadn't heard properly and I asked him what he meant. He said to me again: "I'll donate this house for the Society's work". Not knowing what else to say, I asked a naive question: "And where will you live?" He smiled, because he had two or three other houses, as he explained to me. I left thanking him for everything and returned to the Society, unable to believe my ears.

When I told him what had happened, the Master gave me, for the first time in my discipleship up to then, warm congratulations. He said that I had overcome my resistances, I had opened up my soul, and I had embraced this man with acceptance. And I had expressed to him who I was in relation to the spiritual work which we did at the Society. He then added something which I wasn't expecting: "Now there is no longer any need for you to see your friends to tell them what we have been talking about. You have passed through the field with what happened today."

When all these issues had been settled within me and the importance of the positive thoughts, which had brought an immediate result, had been explained to me again, the burning question of the gift of the house also came up in the conversation. I was filled with enthusiasm for this idea and I was impatient to begin negotiations on putting it into practice. But the position and ideas of a disciple are one thing; those of a Master are another. I shall never in my life forget what I heard at that moment about the gift of the house. Having looked deep into my eyes, the Master said to me: "You must write a letter very soon to this gentleman. You will tell him that you have discussed the matter with your Master and that he thanks him warmly for his offer. You will explain, however, that we can't accept it, because the position of the Master is that it would be right for this house to be used for the work which the gentleman is doing himself. We all know that this man is serving society at a spiritual level. So his house is needed for his work to be carried out and it should not belong to the Society."

I was then plunged into a state of unhappy surprise. I attempted to change his mind, although I knew that there was no chance of that happening, because when he took up a position, that was unshakeable. I said, of course, that it was a shame to lose such an opportunity, that we didn't know whether anything of the sort would ever present itself again, and, above all, I emphasised the fact that in this way the work of the Society and of the Master would not expand.

The Master replied: "The work isn't that of anyone, it is of the Entity, the inner Master. If we think that we are doing something, then we haven't understood that everything is done by the higher self. For the Master, every spiritual work is the same as any other. The Society doesn't want to promote itself at the expense of another spiritual task, such as that which must be carried out in the specific house. What is important is that spirituality should be expressed through all the paths. As to the Society, a suitable building will also come for its work when the time is right. But I see that you are sad, Mrs Klairi. You should meditate on the Master's position, in order to understand its inner significance."

The subject was dropped at that point, and I worked hard on accepting the Master's position. I also worked on stability in reducing the resistances which had caused me so much trouble. The results of the work are obvious. I saw that only if there is acceptance of everything will the resistances leave you and things will sort themselves out of their own accord. I continued to cultivate this acceptance and to develop it within me in the years as a disciple which followed.

DIRECTNESS

Movement, stillness, movement. And the same thing again. Movement, stillness, movement. And I watched, as if I were seeing for the first time something I hadn't seen before. And yet the spectacle was a very common one – two disciples and the Master talking in a corner of the garden. I couldn't hear what they were saying, but I could see their faces and expressions. And I couldn't take my eyes off them. Movement, stillness, movement!

I shook my head in an effort to escape from this invincible fascination. What had happened to me? I lifted the book from the table and began to read again. But some power made me soon put it down again and watch the three who were in conversation. Seeing that I couldn't get away from the need to watch, I wondered what it was which seemed so strange to me. I looked more carefully at the three who were talking and saw great contrasts between them in the way they expressed themselves.

One of the disciples spoke as he always did, with constant changes of expression on his face, with movements of the hands, with bending at the waist. He seemed to bring out all his being through every word which he spoke. The other disciple was the exact opposite. He didn't move his hands, or his body, even his face made very few contortions. I would see that before he uttered a sentence, he would twist his tongue around three times in his mouth and then speak. He was that careful in what he said.

The Master now. Let me see how he expresses himself. His face absolutely calm, so calm that I would say that he isn't listening to what is being said next to him. But he was in fact listening, because suddenly a change came over him. You would say that his face was playing with all forms of human expression, it was as if he was changing masks continuously. Joy, sadness, anger, certainty, and many other emotions. And then calm again, the impression that he wasn't actually there.

As I watched the contrasts between these three individuals, my mind wondered which of them I resembled. I knew the answer: I was like the one who twisted his tongue around in his mouth. And I was like that because I had decided to be so some years before. Before I took that decision, I was like the other disciple, the spontaneous, the demonstrative one. Afterwards, however, when I'd been through many trials in life, I decided not to show my feelings, to be careful about what I said, in case I produced negative impressions in others about me. I didn't like what I was now, but I didn't like what I was before either. I rejected both – the spontaneity and great self-control.

Whenever I asked friends and acquaintances which of the two they thought more correct – whether, that is, one should be spontaneous or reserved in one's expression, I received totally conflicting answers. One of them would say: "I don't really know. But what I like about so-and-so is his spontaneity. He doesn't keep anything to himself, he does whatever occurs to him at the particular moment." But another would intervene: "No, his manner is unacceptable. Does he think at all before he speaks? He ends up talking nonsense." As to those who are very careful in their speech, I also heard differing views. Some thought that those who think a lot before speaking are, deep down, diffident, whereas others maintained that this practice shows seriousness, care, and responsibility.

My reserve in the way in which I spoke and expressed myself generally began to make problems for me when I went to the Society. The other disciples didn't approve of my attitude, but I was unwilling to change it. I had had a number of unpleasant experiences as a result of spontaneity; I didn't need any more. Let them say whatever they want.

Here, however, I must clarify something. When I was with the Master I did not adopt this approach, except in rare instances, as I have said. I was completely spontaneous, I told him whatever came into my mind, what I was feeling, what I desired, or what I repressed. This was because I had realised from the beginning when I got to know him that whatever I said to him, he would accept with understanding. And then I had understood that only if I expressed myself freely, would I receive the answers appropriate to helping me advance in my discipleship. My inclination for learning overcame any possible fears of a rebuke, because, in any event, I saw that a rebuke was also an expression of love and not of rejection.

One day, a disciple brought up the question of my reserve in a group discussion. Frequently, we discussed disciples' problems, except, of course, for individual personal issues, all together in order to find a solution. So this disciple told everybody that I should change, because I was creating problems in my contacts with new members, and with the disciples. I didn't give my own opinion, I didn't take part dynamically. Everybody spoke and a great deal was heard – all of it negative on this subject. Some of them said that I should break down my personality, that I should become something else, that I should forget my old self, and so on. I felt very unhappy with all this criticism of me, and I anxiously awaited the reply of the Master, to whom the problem had been put. Because he also had on many occasions recommended that I should change, I was afraid that he would tell me off again, even if the others were present. But his answer was a deliverance. He said:

"I will say something, to end this subject once and for all, because at other times there have been private conversations about Mrs Klairi's personality. There is no need for her to do any of the things you say. She shouldn't break down her personality, she must only evolve it. In any case, the same applies to all of you. You are all working to overcome your deficiencies. Mrs Klairi is being trained to be more direct and dynamic. To express the power which she conceals within her. So let's not talk any more about the matter, it concerns her own learning process, and the Master is handling this."

The discussion stopped there, and the same issue was never brought up again by anyone. In any event, the Master's words prompted the disciples yet again to look at their own deficiencies and to work to overcome them. Of everything that was said that day, what impressed itself most upon my mind was the word 'direct'. I had to become, he said, direct. But what does directness mean, how is it manifested, and how is it acquired when you don't possess it?

Although the meaning of the word is well known, I opened the dictionary to be more certain, and I read that 'direct' describes something that manifests itself without the mediation of anything. The word has many applications which concern both specific and abstract matters. From the point of view of philosophy, I saw that direct knowledge is that which doesn't use reason but which is revealed intuitively.

But it's one thing to know what directness means, and another to express it. I had to first discover the obstacle to its expression. There was no need for me to look very far, the obstacle was my many thoughts about everything. I thought about everything as though I had nothing else to do from morning till night. In fact, sometimes I was angry with myself and said: 'Stop all the thinking!'. How then was I to be demonstrative with so many thoughts? It was these which kept me closed up, it was these that I had to rid myself of. When I had arrived at this conclusion and was reflecting on how I could reduce my countless thoughts, something happened which made me think about the problem again.

While I was listening to the conversation of a disciple, who was talking very hastily and enthusiastically, the Master said suddenly: "Why are you talking like that? Why don't you use your brain a little? Do you do all your thinking with your belly?". Those words wrecked everything for me. So the girl's haste was also a mistake, just like my own excessive caution. Then what was the right, the direct thing?

Since I had learnt that the belly is in the physical field the equivalent of the emotional sphere, I concluded that any spontaneous, emotional expression is not correct if it is not controlled by the mind. But when the mind restricts emotion, again it's a mistake. Where, then, was I to find the right position, the golden mean? I said nothing to the Master about all these processes. I wanted to arrive somewhere on my own, to find out what directness means. I reflected that, since he teaches us to be direct, this means that he also expresses himself directly. So I began to observe him in all his workings, in order to learn from them. It was a difficult job, of course, because the Master changes his manner of expression every moment.

Sometimes he talks so fast that it's difficult to grasp his meanings. At other times he says only one sentence and then doesn't add a single word, as if he wishes to leave you hanging. Sometimes his face is completely motionless, while at other times it grimaces continually, playing with its every crease, even with the hairs of his head. In watching all this, I began to wonder whether directness might mean the whole of the ceaseless alternations.

One day, when he was making a difficult analysis and the words came out of his mouth in an unbelievable flow, I couldn't resist asking him how he could express his thoughts with such ease. He replied at once: "The Master doesn't think". And then he returned to the subject of the discussion, without saying anything more. Is that what he said? He doesn't think? I'd believed that I had to restrict my thoughts, not that I had to dispense with them completely. How is it possible not to think at all?

While the subject of 'non-thought' was tormenting me, I remembered what the dictionary said: that direct knowledge from a philosophical viewpoint is intuitive knowledge without the mediation of reason. So that was it! The Master is intuitive! This idea fascinated me. At that period I had an astral relation with him, and in spite of the fact that he used to say that he is an ordinary person, I refused to believe it. I wanted to see him as some super-being, with supernatural powers. Because if I saw him like that, then I should be able to rely on him. I didn't want him an ordinary human being, like all the rest.

The fact that he didn't think, or at least so I had understood from his words, confirmed my idea of him. "He may say that he's like everybody else", I thought; "he says that out of modesty." I kept him at the exalted height which I wanted, and I was very pleased with the position I'd given him.

On the day when he told me that he didn't think, something happened which proved to me yet again the existence of the diffused consciousness, of the wisdom which watches over everything, guiding man out of his errors. Because it was a case of error, of my imagination, in which I wanted to turn the Master into a god, it was like this that I needed him. So as I was living in my magic, a disciple went up to the Master, asked him a specific question, and he replied "Wait a minute, let me think, and I'll give you an answer". Disillusionment! The idol was thrown down from its pedestal, and I saw the Master as an ordinary human being like the rest of us. And I began to think that in the end I shouldn't believe him, since he said one thing one moment and another the next. How could he not think and also think?

Years passed before I realised what he meant by these opposing concepts. When he said that he didn't think, he was referring to the inner Master, who brought out through his mouth the flow of the inner word. But when he said that he had to think, he was referring to the human self, which used the specific mental equipment to give the – also specific – reply which the disciple wanted.

But I couldn't understand any of this at that time, and so I remained in a state of disillusionment for some days. Now I know from experience that the direct Word can be expressed even by a disciple. Of course, directness has to do with the work he has done to begin to express it and with the union which he builds each time by means of a more expanded, a higher field of consciousness, to which it refers. Trained disciples, for example, when they are giving meditation to a group, don't think about their words; these simply flow, they are expressed without thinking by their mind. Because the Master is constantly in union with the higher self, this is the reason why he doesn't think when delivering a teaching. But when he has to deal with a lower mental field, he uses thought, as everyone does.

When the first disillusionment had subsided within me during those days, I began again to observe the Master's manner of expression. I had noticed, in the months when I was learning, that a characteristic of his way of working was direct responsiveness to whoever or whatever came to seek his help. His manner of operation was not always a piece of advice or a specific teaching, it was also very simple practical issues. At the time, for example, when we were painting the Society's premises, because no one was able to open a bucket of paint, he found a tool and opened it himself. Similar occurrences took place very frequently. I saw that he functioned as though nothing intervened between himself and the object of his work, the individual who was asking him something, the need which arose on each occasion. He was always direct without the enthusiasms of spontaneity, but also without the reservations which arise from a multitude of thoughts. Thus, although his face changed expression every moment, even if he was thinking or not thinking, directness remained his chief characteristic.

My feelings about the directness of the Master were mixed. Enclosed within my inhibitions and distressed by the negative impressions of my past spontaneity, sometimes I admired the way he worked and sometimes I envied him. I wanted to become direct, plain, responsive to everything, and yet something was stopping me.

As I couldn't find any other way of solving my problem, I decided to meditate on the issue of directness, and of spontaneity, and of reserve. In order to assist me in the work I was doing, I chose three individuals who represented these methods of functioning; I projected their figures before me, and united myself with their inner field. The answers came quickly, as though it was something very simple which was waiting for me to look for it so that it could reveal itself.

I first brought to mind that disciple who, as I knew, was always spontaneous. I saw that within his body there were various forms of energy, chiefly in his head and solar plexus. These energies seemed to come from within him and to be constantly poured outwards. When this happened, the disciple experienced relief and became inert, as though he'd fallen into a sleep. Later, when new thoughts and emotions flooded him, he wanted again to be rid of them, in the belief that in this way he could relax.

Of course, he didn't relax, except for a short time, because new currents were constantly passing through him, causing upheaval, which forced him all the time to get it out of his system. I understood immediately that this kind of spontaneity is the result of fear, that man does not know what to do with the currents which flood him and which cause him congestion when he keeps them within himself.

The second person I studied was the disciple who didn't find it easy to be demonstrative. I also saw in him also similar powers within him, only he didn't allow them to manifest themselves. I noticed that whenever any of these was expressed, he took up a defensive stance, as if he were afraid that another, negative, power would enter to fill the empty place of the energy which had been externalised. And so he preferred to keep the currents which were known to him and familiar within his vehicle, rather than risk their replacement by others more unpleasant. That is to say, in the second case also, the cause was fear.

Then I started to meditate on the Master. I saw that in his physical, his emotional, and his mental body, absolute calm prevailed. If a current passed through him, this was assimilated by the calm and was externalised again as calm, which took different forms: it became speech, action, movement. The same happened with both positive and negative currents; everything was calmed and transformed, to be expressed directly in the way that it should. I realised that this was the explanation for the constant changes in his expression, and his actions generally. I saw that through stability in calmness, he was able directly to express what the other person needed, to convey to him his own serenity. If someone, for example, brought him a current of sorrow, this was transmuted into calm, as the opposite – joy, optimism, hope – was projected by the Master. Thus a balance was achieved in the saddened person, and, naturally, without the Master's calm being lost. As I went more deeply into him, I discerned a total absence of fear of all the currents. He was not closed into these, as the disciple before had been, but always accepted them calmly. Nor did he attempt to rid himself of the forces and energies which passed through him; the only thing which he did was to transform them all into calm. Fear did not exist within the Master!

Since the findings of this meditation seemed strange to me, because it wasn't easy for me to accept a state without fear, I decided to break my silence and to ask the Master if he felt fear or not. His words were as follows: "The Master does not fear, because he is united with God. He does not fear because he doesn't regard himself as something special, he doesn't regard himself as even existing. For the Master, the only one who exists is the Entity, God. So what is he to fear? He has nothing to lose, because he doesn't have anything. For that reason he is direct, because he is united, nothing else intervenes, no fear, between the Master and God."

This answer was, of course, of the greatest importance. I saw how far distant I was from the state of fearlessness, and, while I understood that a life without any fear at all would be superb, I couldn't see in any way how I could pass into such a field of consciousness. The Master again gave me an optimistic message, which has helped me ever since then whenever a new fear makes its appearance. He said:

"All disciples – and the whole of humanity – will overcome their fears one day. But until that happens, you must work steadily for the reduction of fear, and this will gradually bring about its complete dissolution. And it will bring it about because fearlessness is the true nature of man, it is the pure entity, which without inhibitions is expressed directly and in the same way towards everything. Meditate, Mrs Klairi, invoke the power of the higher self, and perform service. This is the path to fearlessness and directness."

SEXUAL RELATIONS

"Today, Master, I want us to have a discussion about a matter which concerns me a great deal".

"Of course, Mrs Klairi. What is this matter?"

"It is people's sexual relations. As I am now talking everyday to lots of people, I notice that the chief problem is in the relations of man and woman, even if it shows itself in some other way. And this surprises me."

"But I told you so some time ago, if you remember. I told you that when you begin to converse with people, you will see that the cause of the problems is basically in sexual relations. And you replied that you found this an exaggeration, because there are, as you said at the time, a thousand and one other problems in humanity."

"Yes, Master, I have remembered your words, and my own objection. But now I see that you were right, but I never cease to be surprised each time I discover the same problem. I couldn't have imagined that sex creates so many difficulties."

"It isn't exactly sex that creates them; it's the attitude of man towards it."

"Yes, of course, but why should there be such an attitude?"

"Would you like to tell me something more concrete, so I can see what sort of thing you are talking about?"

"Where shall I start, Master, there are so many... One lady, married 20 years, told me the other day that she has never felt sexual pleasure. A young man around 30 admitted to me that he has never made love. A young girl told me that she wants to change lovers all the time, but that none of them meets her emotional needs. Ah, yes. A gentleman of around 40 maintains that he has outgrown sexual needs and concerns himself only with spiritual matters. And a woman who was complaining of pains in the ovaries, when I asked her what her sex life is like, told me that she hadn't come to the Society to consult a sexologist, but to receive spiritual healing."

"I can understand, Mrs Klairi, that all this comes as a surprise to you, but this is the reality. In a little while you'll know what answer and what guidance to give in such cases. The issue of sex is much misunderstood. But tell me, when they say things such as you have quoted, do you ask why these things are happening?"

"Of course I ask, and, what is more, their answers are always in my mind, as I try to find a solution. I can tell you them, if you like."

"Please do so."

"The married lady told me that her husband is to blame for her problem because he isn't in the slightest bit tender. The young man said that girls today are superficial and artificial, and he doesn't want them. The young woman who changes her lovers maintains that her ideal has not yet been found. The one who doesn't make love says that he considers sex inferior and bestial. And when I asked him what happens with his wife, he replied that he tries to bring her to his way of thinking, but she is irritable all the time and takes no notice of him. As to the lady with the pains, I didn't ask her anything more, because she immediately closed the conversation. But there are other cases, Master, I've only told you a few."

"Alright, those are enough. I see then a common characteristic in the things you've spoken about. Have you perhaps realised what that is?"

"How should I know? The denial of sex, perhaps? But the girl doesn't deny it; she wants it very much. What else do they have in common? A difficulty in contact? No? It isn't these things?"

"It is these things, but the common feature in all of them is that they displace the problem on to others, and don't look to see whether it's inside themselves. Except, of course, for the lady with the pains who refused to answer you, all the others do the same thing. Even the one who no longer wants sexual contact adopts this attitude, as he said, because sex is bestial, and not because he himself has this attitude towards sex."

"Do you mean, then, that in reality the problem is only in each one of them and not in their partner?"

"Not exactly. But it is in each of them, as well as in their partner, as well as in the whole of society. It is a human problem which is given expression by everybody. And its cause is not what shows itself, it's much deeper."

"What is its cause, Master?"

"It is again what crops up in all manifestations, man's refusal of union. Because union, albeit only with his partner, is a broadening of the ego, which, however, presupposes a dissolution of the individual ego."

"Yes, but sex is not something unpleasant, so that you wouldn't want it. On the contrary, it is gratification, happiness, completeness."

"Naturally it is, but the unconscious fear of the loss of the separate ego is often much stronger than the desire for sexual enjoyment."

"The fear which you speak of supplies an answer in the case of those who refuse sex, or who don't find pleasure in it. But how is the opposite explained, why it is that the young girl who wants to make love constantly is not satisfied, and feels that no one gives her the emotion which she seeks?"

"This girl also has the same fear. She wishes to take from her partners, but she does not give her self, her soul. And she doesn't do this, of course, because she wants to remain in her own individualistic field, in her personal ego."

"But she maintains that she gives everything, but no one responds to her giving."

"That's what she thinks. Her giving contains a great need, a demand, I would say, that the other person should give her something in exchange. Her demand repels the men who get close to her for a little while, and that is why she can't create a stable relationship."

"Do you think she's a nymphomaniac?"

"No, I didn't say anything like that. Although she may be. But what is certainly happening in her case is that she seeks to be given to. And what she is seeking is not necessarily sexual pleasure, it may be much more loving care, interest, and so on."

"Very well, but isn't it entirely natural that there should be such a need?"

"It is natural, but it ties you down. Man is tormented by his needs. And so only when he changes his approach and begins to give without caring whether he will meet with a response is it possible for him to live his whole life dynamically, including sex, of course."

"What you are saying applies to all the teaching on love, giving, service. What have these got to do with sex?"

"Isn't sex life? If it is life, shouldn't the one teaching which covers everything be applied to it as well?"

"You're right in saying that we are being trained in the teaching of synthesis, since this, the sexual element, is included in the training."

"Why do you have doubts, Mrs Klairi? What does Plato say in the Symposium about sexual love?"

"Yes, all that is well known. He speaks of 'eros' towards all of life, towards what is fine, sublime, formless, which leads to the Absolute. But here we're not talking about the concepts which Socrates supplied, but about the simple relations between a couple."

"Don't look upon the two things as being different. They're the same. If the man doesn't love the woman and if the woman doesn't adore the man, how will they be prepared for union with the Absolute?"

"So sex is a preparation, it isn't an end in itself?"

"Sex leads to the union of souls, so that they can advance to union with the Spirit, with the Entity. The more this happens, the more sex is transformed into adoration, into ecstasy."

"Master, I'm tired. I see that I can't give any practical advice to anybody in order to help them. They must receive all the teaching which you give yourself. And this takes years. But how many are interested in such a learning experience? And then, why should they be interested, when they're in a state of tension, when they're quarrelling from morning till night, when their nerves are on edge, or they are physically ill? Much they care about whether they'll arrive at the Absolute which Socrates talks about."

"Do you know why you're tired now, Mrs Klairi?"

"I suppose because I was afraid of the volume of the work and the refusal of people to work for it."

"No, Mrs Klairi. Over and above what you have said, you are tired because you want your words at all costs to produce a result. But that isn't your role, it's no business of yours whether others will change. You simply give them certain items of knowledge which you have received from the Master and they make use of them as they wish. Calm down a little, unite yourself with the inner Master, to enable us to continue the discussion. Give the Master the problem and leave him to solve it. Enter into meditation."

I followed his advice, I relaxed, I calmed down, and I allowed the problem to be settled by the higher self. The Master, next to me, sang ritual songs to help me to emerge from the tension and to see things more simply. As these songs speak of God and the spiritual powers within man, in a few minutes my mood had changed, and then the Master said:

"What happened to you before happened because you have not yet acquired enough experience of the way in which you must handle things. For that reason we'll discuss what's worrying you, until it no longer causes such difficulties. But now I want to reply to something you said before: that you can't give any practical advice so that people are helped in their sexual relations. You're wrong, a lot can be done with an opinion about a practical application which the other person probably hasn't thought of on his own. If he is a disciple, then we analyse the problem at length, we give him a meditation on his subject, we set him to observe his reactions, and so on. If, however, he isn't a disciple, then, for the present at least, we give him just a few items which he can use correctly and easily."

"And so to the woman who says that her husband is not tender what can I say, when she comes back?"

"Tell her that her refusal to take pleasure in sex is a kind of punishment which she unconsciously imposes on her husband, because he doesn't behave in a tender manner towards her. But this punishment also means for herself the deprivation of a sex life. Then you can tell her to try herself to be very tender with him, so as to convey to him a current of the tenderness which he lacks. And this she can do at any moment, there's no need to wait for sexual contact. Tenderness expresses itself with a smile, with a few words, with interest in everything. If you see that she doesn't want to listen to you, tell her to give it a try, to see if she feels better. All these things – and many others, of course – are simple pieces of advice which may help a person."

"I wish that you would give me similar opinions on all the cases which I've told you of, Master. I think that will help me to see the matter globally. For example, what am I to say to the young man who has never made love?"

"I think his problem is purely emotional. For various reasons, this man does not believe in himself, he imagines that women don't like him, that he's probably impotent, that he won't manage it. He doesn't know this, or even if he knows it, he refuses to admit it to himself. Thus his rejection of his own person he turns into rejection of all women, in order to be relieved of the tension of soul which self-rejection causes in him. He must, therefore, have an analysis made for him, so he can see the truth. And then you must make him remember moments in his life when he has proved that he is capable, strong, worthy, so that he can see that he isn't a failure. Finally, you should tell him to have various girls for ordinary company and companionship, until be becomes familiar with the female sex, and then the sexual relationship which he wants will come. Naturally, it would be a good idea for you to see him a number of times, so you can discuss developments and his difficulties."

"In the case of the girl with her many friends, you don't need to tell me anything. I can carry out the analysis which you told me of before – that she is constantly in search of something – and tell her that she must begin to give. Isn't that so?"

"Quite right! Now we come to the one who refuses sex, because he thinks it inferior. It appears from what he says that this person has some preliminary training in spiritual matters. Consequently, you can speak to him on another level. You can explain to him that the sex life binds a person to the instinctive function only when he abandons himself to the currents of desire and gratification. If, however, in parallel with the sex life he also works for spirituality, then there is no danger of polarisation. On the other hand, denial of sex is a denial of union with a part of life and, naturally, someone who does not unite himself with everything cannot advance spiritually. As to his claim that he has overcome any sexual need, tell him that this happens in very advanced individuals, initiates and sages. Man frequently suppresses a desire, thinking that it doesn't exist within him, but in essence he hasn't been delivered from it, he's simply burying it and refusing to see it."

"I think the case of this man is more difficult than the previous ones, because he doesn't see his problem, he thinks that he is fine. And as to his wife, he says only that she is not sufficiently evolved, because she doesn't agree with his views. However, I will speak to him in the way that you have said."

"And so now there is only the woman with pains in her ovaries. Do you know what you must say to her?"

"I think I do. I shall explain to her the direct connection of her illness with the retentions of energy in the body. Then, depending on what she tells me, I will adapt the reply in the light of what we have said today."

"Very good. Now I will give you certain facts so that you can study them and be able to answer appropriately when there is a need. Sex is life, desire for life, for union. Sex is sacred, because without it the universe wouldn't exist, there would be no creation, pulsation, harmony, music. Every pulsation in nature is a tremor, an erotic game which vibrates beings to unite with one another, and, as they unite, to be united with God. Man's problem is his need to be polarised to the dense vibrations of the body, and not to extend himself to other subtle fields of vibration of the spirit. He forgets that his being is not only a body; it is a soul and spirit. And so he becomes attached to his own body, or to the body of his partner and does not allow himself to function spiritually.

"Each man and each woman at the time when they make love must see first the entity within their partner and then the body. Thus, while they will also live through the body, they will not be polarised to it. Sex is of the soul, even if it is expressed physically. Because the body is the tool of the soul, the form of the spirit. Man's fear of sex is the result of the need of the soul to escape from the bonds of matter and of form. The soul seeks the freedom of the spirit and the body enslaves it. But if man does not recognise the spirit within the body, if he doesn't see that this also is sacred and holy, deliverance will not come.

"The role of the two sexes is a supreme role. Because man and woman are the expression in form of the opposing forces which have to be united and amalgamated, one within the other. Only when this becomes consciousness and life experience will man reach fulfilment and union with God. Everything I have said today is a subject for meditation. But that's enough for the moment. The issue which you have raised today is a very broad one and we shall talk about it many more times. Begin now to apply what we have said and keep me informed of the results."

I thanked the Master for these first instructions on sexual relations. I sensed the range of this topic, which we did in fact discuss repeatedly in the years which followed, until it was completely clear within me. In the meantime, I began to put into practice his advice with the people I was seeing. As I became firmly established in the position on the importance of sex, things became very simple. People's objections became fewer as I learnt to see the causes of their problems. Often, simple advice brought positive results and, moreover, led some of these people to the decision to work systematically on self-knowledge. Of course, there are always cases where no will for change is expressed. Then I leave the matter to the consciousness of each individual, and I don't wish a result to be achieved at all costs as I did at the beginning.

I shall refer frequently to the subject of sex, because it is, as I have said, a vital problem of our society; a problem with many aspects which have been brought to the level of consciousness – and many which haven't.

DISILLUSIONMENTS

First, second, third, fourth... and then I stopped counting. I had realised that these would be countless. The falls, I mean, the moments of despair, the disillusionments. And all this in the first weeks of my discipleship. But I stayed on; I didn't leave. And I wondered why. What did I want with such a discipleship? Before I got into this channel, it wasn't as though I didn't have my bad times, but, after all, these were within natural limits, at long intervals. Months would pass before a new crisis of melancholy, a difficult time, would come. But what was happening inside me from the time that I became a disciple was something indescribable. It was as though

I'd become a little ball which unseen powers threw sometimes up and sometimes down. And yet I carried on...

"Is this how it is with all the disciples?" I asked myself. And whenever I was feeling calm, I watched the others. I saw that in all of them similar swings made their appearance, but they didn't need to have so much tension, nor to show themselves with so much frequency. Reactions, fatigue, and problems broke out in dependence on the individual characteristics of each of them.

One day, the Master made an analysis on the subject of such changing states in the disciple: "Everything that happens in the Society", he told us at that time, "is exactly similar to everything that happens in life, in the world generally. The group of disciples is a group of people which, naturally, represents humanity. Each one of you conceals within him all human weaknesses, but also all human powers. The difference from other groups of individuals who co-exist in professional, family, social contexts is the presence of the Master, of the consciousness which is rising up within you.

"This consciousness speeds up the rhythm of the work which, albeit unconsciously, every human being does, in order to learn who he is, to get to know his self. So it is very natural that the revelations of contrary aspects within you should occur very frequently, and that they should be intense and painful. But in this way we save time, and time is important at this particular period. There is, you see, a great need for spirituality to be developed, to balance the negative currents which prevail on the planet. The Master asks pardon from the disciples for the pain which he causes them and for the pressure which he sometimes exerts upon them. If we lived in another age, it's probable that the rate of learning would be slower and the problems more gentle. But today the planet is in danger, mankind is going astray, and for this reason we are forced to hurry, to build up spiritual people who will work for the good of everybody. But it won't be always like this. As you become firmly established in the position of a disciple, things will change. Now we have to win time. This is why I often say that one year with the Master is equivalent to ten years' learning in life without a Master. So be patient and everything will soon change for you."

And, in fact, the day came – but only after five or six years – when the Master said: "We're in no hurry, Mrs Klairi. Now the consciousness of the disciple has developed. Things have changed from what they were at the beginning." The strange thing was that when I heard these words, I was not particularly pleased. I wanted the rapid rhythm to continue; I wanted the teaching to spread to large numbers of people, for substantive changes to take place in many. But the Master said that this shouldn't concern me; if the disciple is there, his sequel always comes.

In the early months of my discipleship I was unable to imagine how every fall and rise of mine was related to the whole of humanity. I had no idea about the collective unconscious, about the interaction of all individual forces. Nor did I have, of course, any particular interest in other people, apart from the small circle of family and friends. This interest developed much later. The correlation of individual evolution with the problem of the planet was for me a matter of incomprehensible concepts at that time.

In the meantime, the falls continued. In the pages of the file which I wrote in the early days are scattered sentences, written in between analyses and descriptions. I say somewhere: "I don't know what's happening to me. Suddenly I lose my lucidity of mind, I can't think". Further down I add: "I can't stand it, don't press me so hard, Master. I want a little time." I often felt that my brain couldn't take in any more concepts, and I was seized with despair. How was I to fill so many gaps in my knowledge? And I asked myself: "But why don't I believe what I'm taught, since I've realised that I know all this deep down, I know it intuitively?" As the days passed and new difficulties presented themselves, I began to be possessed by a fear – the fear of rejection. "I'm afraid", I wrote, "that if I don't live up to what I have to do, the Master will turn me out, the other disciples will no longer accept me. How long are they going to wait, how long is the Master going to squander his time and his powers on me?" I didn't suspect at that time that a human being's patience can be inexhaustible.

It was with the help of the inner Master that my problem in grasping the new concepts which I was learning was dealt with. Soon, as I explain in the book on Spiritual Healing, I began to feel that major processes were taking place in my brain. Energies passed within it and vibrated certain centres, as if these were carrying out preliminary work so that I could learn more easily. The pulsation became particularly strong when I was meditating, when I had the feeling that something was constantly entering my skull. Sometimes this reminded me of a drill, sometimes of the powerful rays of the sun, and sometimes it was like a diamond which was glittering on my forehead, spreading light all around me. And all this activation of the brain gradually reduced my problem in grasping new concepts. I began not to be so tired, to understand more quickly everything that I was being taught. Naturally, I didn't realise at the time what had happened. I had no knowledge of the inner consciousness which responds to every need, which penetrates, I would say, into the unconscious, in order to stimulate it. Since I then had a problem in the specific mind, it began to expand, in order for me to take in the teaching of the particular items of knowledge of which I stood in such need.

But man is not only thoughts and ideas. He is also emotions and a body. These were not helped straightaway; they had to go round in many circles, to acquire many experiences for a difference to be made to them. Thus, whenever a doubt appeared about what I was learning, or a resistance to implementing it, things got worse and I felt dreadful. At one such moment, when I had been influenced by the negative ideas of an acquaintance about the truth of the teaching and the genuineness of the Master, I suddenly felt great exhaustion, which lasted for many hours. And I then wrote: "I have been through a very severe crisis. Since yesterday evening I haven't been able to concentrate my gaze anywhere. And all night, instead of resting, I became even more tired. In the morning, in the street, I crawled along, my feet heavy; life was empty, my existence insipid. And I was feeling dizzy continually, and wanted to sit down so that I didn't fall." At such difficult times, my refuge was meditation. This gave me back balance and I continued the intensive discipleship which I needed so much.

But the Master was in a hurry, as I said. Firm establishment had to come; the stable state of the spiritual person, the disciple, had to be gained. But I was also in a hurry, I wanted to escape from the swings and the problems. And I wrote at that time: "Why am I in a hurry? Really, why am I? This haste is tiring me and, in the end,

I remain unsatisfied." But soon I again threw myself vigorously into the task of self-knowledge.

How cruel, how discouraging it was for me to discover that I am a very minor human being with enormous weaknesses, with many needs, with great egoism... One by one the negative characteristics of human nature come to break down the illusions of the ego. I wanted notice to be taken of me, always to have a special position. I engaged in self-congratulation whenever I managed to do something good. I fed my self-centredness with my own thoughts. And then I despaired over this wretched state of affairs. I imagined that there was nobody else with so many faults. And then I would get a headache, my stomach would tighten, and I would actually become ill.

I remember that one day I suddenly had a temperature. I got into bed, so that I could stop bothering about anything. The inner torment, the constant swings had worn me out. I telephoned to the Society and told some disciple that I was ill and that they should not expect me. This indisposition seemed like a gift to me; in this way I could be relieved for a little while from the teaching, from the constant pressures to which my ego was subjected as soon as I entered the Society. I had a right at last to rest for a bit.

While I was enjoying the warmth of the bed and abandoning myself to nestling in my enfeeblement, the telephone rang, and the Master's voice said: "What are you doing there, Mrs Klairi?" "I'm ill, Master." "Get up and come to the Society immediately." "But I have a temperature." "It's nothing. When you go out, it will pass." "I can't, Master. I'm burning and my legs are shaking." "Did you hear what I said to you? Get up and come at once. The temperature is from the astral field which you've allowed to overwhelm you."

I got up with unbelievable dejection, without understanding what something astral had to do with the high temperature. Within me I was feeling like swearing at him, like hitting him on the head, like getting rid of his teaching. I'd never known such an oppressor in my life. He doesn't even allow you to be ill!

I dragged myself to the car, I drove very slowly, I climbed the stairs to the Society out of breath. The Master looked at me and said: "Sit down for a little beside me." I slumped into a chair, incapable of doing anything. In a little while I began to perspire. My eyes began to open and my mood to change. I realised that I was undergoing healing. I felt confidence again. Since the Master was concerning himself with me, this meant that I wasn't so awful, that there still was hope. When I had recovered completely, he analysed for me the fever which I had had.

"Every fever is a defence of the organism, it creates combustions for the germs to be burnt up. But apart from the germs and the viruses, there are also minor forces, the negative factors which invade man. These are doubts, desires, and the various egoistic manifestations. As you have been led astray by these and have allowed them to overwhelm you, you became a victim of the astral, of your unsatisfied desires. The fever came to burn up for you these minor forces, as it burns up germs. I told you to come to the Society in order for me to speed up your healing, so that the combustions would happen quickly, since you were unable to perform self-healing on your own. Now, after the spiritual healing, you are well. But you must develop greater resistance, and not let a thought or a few words put you off course. Only then will you not have such collapses, you will not be ill."

Quieter days followed this lesson; there was a greater will on my part to deal with the problems. Of course, the resistances of the personality did not end because I had undergone a healing. And so the declines continued, bringing every so often new disillusionments, but then bringing back the new corresponding inner processes. And there were also, naturally, good moments. I had begun to carry out self-healing and to have impressive results. I had also started to be more direct in the things that happened to me. When something began to bother me, I studied it mentally and through meditation, so as not to let it dominate me. But the Master was not content with these changes, because his objective was, as it is of every Master, the constant broadening of the disciple's consciousness. As soon as I had made one transition, before I was even well and truly grounded in that, he would immediately give me the next one. And so he helped me to be in a state of constant alertness. Naturally, in order to achieve each new conquest, I passed through various positive and negative stages, with the related declines and disappointments.

One of the problems which the Master pointed out to me at that time was that I continued to be excessively concerned with my own self. For a long time my meditations were about my personal needs, as I have already said. My attitude at the Society was egocentric. He told me repeatedly that it was a great mistake for me to receive so much energy and not to diffuse it to others, not to perform a corresponding service. It was only then that I began to stand on my own feet, it was only then that I had started to understand the basic meanings of the teaching. In order to avoid doing what he told me, I resorted again to meditation, in the hope obtaining from that some different direction. I called upon some entity to come and support me, but the voice of my consciousness told me: “You must obey the Master”.

And the new decline would begin. Distrust, depression, negation, and a constant feeling that I was unworthy to be a disciple. And these things became more intense every time that I was unwilling to do something for others. Until, one day, I decided to ignore all the difficulties and simply to profess myself to be a disciple, in spite of everything that was happening to me. But I wondered whether the Master accepted as a disciple someone who hid within herself so little good and so much that was negative. I wrote my thoughts in the file and read them to the Master and his wife, who was with us at that time. Two and a half months had passed since I started my discipleship. In that period, respect for the entity of the Master had developed and my position, the disposition of my soul, had firmly established itself. In spite of this, I knew that I had to make this statement, to express in words my inner decision.

The Master accepted me then as a disciple because what is always of importance is the individual's inclination and not his problems. Problems persist until the last moment, before the transition to total union with God. And, moreover, he immediately gave me a new pattern of meditation, which I worked with for a very long period. Through that pattern I received a major teaching on the role which anyone who devotes himself to a spiritual task must have – a role of a celebrant, one who expresses the Entity, who decides to work for the spread of spirituality.

"Master, don't you have problems?" new disciples would ask, when they had acquired a certain amount of boldness with him.

"No, the Master has no problem. Why should he have?"

"And when you happen to fall ill, don't you see the illness as a problem?"

"The physical body is subject to the laws of nature. I do what I have to do about it, but the Master doesn't have a problem."

"And when you are in some unpleasant place, where, for example, there's a lot of noise, doesn't that annoy you?"

"The Master sees in all noises, as in everything else, an expression of the Entity. And for precisely that reason he has absolutely no problem."

"That is to say that you never experience disillusionment, whatever happens?"

"Disillusionment, disappointment presupposes the existence of some allure, some magic, a strong attraction to something. But since for the Master all things are alike, and he isn't attracted to one thing more than he is attracted to another, he can't be disappointed by anything. Quite simply, in everything, even in those things which seem negative, he recognises the Entity."

"And so why then do you urge us so often to concern ourselves with different things when you say that all things are the same?"

"Precisely because of what I've said. So you can see that all things are the same."

"And so our disappointments and falls are due only to preferences?"

"But isn't that the way it is? As long as you want to only be strong, for example, you deny the fact that you are also weak. This disappoints you whenever it shows itself and you go into decline. You don't accept both aspects of your self and for that reason they are not harmonised inside you."

"But how do you stand an expression of timidity or fear?"

"By ceasing to see it coloured as timidity and fear, and by seeing these as small manifestations of your overall power. Just as you accept the existence of the cells which all together structure your body, so you should also accept the other small parts of your self. Then there will be no problem."

"But you always point out our mistakes to us and say that we shouldn't have falls."

"Yes, that's the way it is, until you see that a mistake is a mistake for as long as it confines you within its small limited power, thus causing falls. But when you understand that the small is a part of the great, then you will not be restricted, you won't be led astray by this. You will have no problem."

"The conclusion from what you say is that, in the end, disillusionments are artificial, in essence, they don't exist."

"Disappointments and enthusiasms are the result of limited awareness. When the mind is broadened, these are dissolved, and only true nature remains, the great ontological existence, which is free within all things, since it handles them all without the slightest problem."

As my personal disappointments became rarer, I began to observe the other disciples, and to see their reactions. The shared characteristic of them all was that each decline was always related to one of their own personal problems. If the problem involved another situation, a difficult family situation, for example, no collapse came, but various other reactions, such as rage, anxiety, distress. Thus I soon realised that the fall of man is individual, even if it expresses the collective unconscious. And this happens because, deep down, we are all looking for evolution, and we all suffer when we are unable to make progress.

I can remember a young disciple who had great aptitude of soul, but because of her age and external circumstances, she was unable to stabilise her position. Every so often she was distracted by her weakness and was seized with despair. Sometimes she did what everybody does: she shifted the blame on to the Master and found fault with him for the instructions which he had given her. At other times, however, she didn't have the strength of character even to find excuses, and then she became a wreck because of her despair. Her expressive face was impaired, withered, and her youthful features aged as a result of their mournful expression.

One day I went to speak to the Master and saw this disciple sitting on a chair, wearing the familiar despairing expression. I always felt sorry for her when she was like this, because I knew from personal experience what she was feeling. I sat down to see what would happen and looked at the Master, whose face was calm, as if he felt nothing. But he was talking to her constantly in order to bring her out of her depression. That time, nothing special had happened; it was simply that so many small and successive difficulties in putting the teaching into practice had accumulated that the disciple had reached the conclusion that she was useless and incompetent, and that she ought to withdraw from discipleship.

The Master talked, analysed, passed to her some strong current, but nothing changed. Her posture was the same: a body slack upon the seat, a sad face which nothing could alter. Then the Master started to talk to her about great entities, saints, spiritual beings, and he told her to begin to envision them. So great was her need to escape from the problem that she didn't resist this flow and in a few minutes was immersed in a meditation, one of the most important that she had practised so far – as she herself told us. I can't give many details of this meditation, for the reasons I have explained, but I will mention only one other thing. When the girl saw the spiritual beings and when she had been calmed by their presence, the Master told her to see herself among them. When the meditation finished, she told us that in this distance which she had crossed in her consciousness there were no separations, but everybody and everything was alike. This experience was very substantive for the disciple, because it showed her that, although she had many weaknesses, she was at the same time a spiritual being with great possibilities. Her faith in herself was renewed and she continued on the course of her discipleship.

When I was alone with the Master, I asked him how he was able to transform the great suffering of the disciple into ecstasy, because it was ecstasy that we were talking about. He replied: “Mrs Klairi, the role of the Master is to make use of the error, to break down the limitation, to broaden the consciousness. A person who sees his limited self only is in error. This disciple had fallen into such debilitation because she had entirely forgotten, had ignored her strong aspect, her entity. The greater the error is, the greater need the soul has to overcome it. For this reason the Master gave her a correspondingly large ontological field, so that balance would come, so that she would emerge from the small view of herself and pass over to the other, the real one.”

Utilisation of error, then, I thought at the time. Not an outcry, not condemnation, but a simple balancing with what is correct. Until there is no error, as the Master says. I had, however, a second question, and I asked it at once. “Didn't you feel sorry for her when she was in such a dreadful state before? I saw that you were very calm. Indeed, for a moment I was angry, because you seemed to me cold and indifferent. So aren't you sorry for anyone?"

The Master smiled at the question, which showed that I was never going to leave him alone if what a 'Master' means was not completely cleared up in my mind. This, in any event, was what I continued to do in the years which followed: to ask about, to investigate his ontological field, until I understood what it was. That day he told me: "The Master both pities and doesn't pity, because he is united with the people he is sorry for. He takes this current into himself, but not in order to identify with it. He takes it into himself in order to transform it into power, into love. Since, then, this transformation happens instantaneously, pity ceases to exist for the Master and becomes love, it becomes the highest field of consciousness. The pity of man is due to the fact that he does not know or forgets this field, his entity."

There was within me at that moment another question, but I didn't dare to put it into words. I wondered why he hadn't given to me – up to that time, of course – a similar field of ecstatic meditation. A certain jealousy sprang up inside me, which grew stronger during the days which followed, as I saw that the young disciple retained the state which she had experienced. It seems that the same current of jealousy spread to the whole group, and whereas the Master said that we must think of the transition of each disciple as the transition of the whole group, each of us wanted it for himself, to experience the satisfaction, the deliverance, the ecstasy himself. Years passed before I began to make this state a reality within myself. To see, I mean, any pleasure of another as my own, to experience in my own self the evolution of each disciple, to be ecstatic with his ecstasy. But at that time it was very difficult for me to experience being at one and to understand the workings of the Master. I thought that he too had favourites among the disciples, which was, of course, a very natural thing to happen to me, because I had not advanced to the assimilation of all things which he taught us every day.

One disciple, also a very young girl, couldn't endure the transition of the other disciple and one day told the Master that she was in despair about herself. She wasn't consciously telling lies, she believed that she really was in a terrible state. But this belief of hers was the product of her mind, and stemmed from her jealousy, because she too wanted to experience ecstasy.

The Master saw at once the motive of this disciple, as he told me in a conversation later on, but he let her live through all the experience, for her to understand her error. She began to meditate, sitting next to him, and projected before herself the entities which the other disciple had projected. When the meditation ended, she was in no particular state of happiness, being somehow satisfied, but at the same time, somehow disappointed. The Master then explained to her that her meditation was astral: it had been produced by her jealousy and her desire to reach the level of the other disciple. It was not a pure disposition of soul and for that reason did not lead her to real union. The girl denied the existence of the astral, objected to the analysis, and many days had to pass for her to understand and accept the existence of the jealousy. And then, of course, she fell into true disillusionment. But the Master didn't give her the same pattern to help her, because for the special case of each disciple many ways of teaching can be given. But to each is given what he should receive, and not what he believes is right.

In observing the Master, who always continued to be a mysterious being for me, I saw that he really didn't go into declines, he was not disappointed by anything. I often looked at him when something unpleasant was happening, to catch him out, to seize on his current of despair. But I never managed it! And so I can't say anything about the disillusionments of the Master. What can I say about something that is non-existent? The Master is not disillusioned because, quite simply, he has no illusions. He is master of the opposites and is in constant harmony with everything. And this he teaches to all alike, without preferences and distinctions.

HOPE AND UNION

"Every miracle takes three days, and the biggest, four". These wise words of the Greek proverb came to my mind again and again when, years ago, something happened to me which at that time I regarded as astonishing. This event occurred a few months after my resignation from the school where I was working as an infant teacher. And it happened a few months before I met the Master.

At that period I used to paint many hours each day, and I was very pleased with this occupation. I was now free of professional obligations, with children old enough to have taken a substantive part of their responsibilities upon themselves, and I could make use of my time in whatever way I wished. And so I painted, and wondered what I was going to do with the pictures which had accumulated in my room. I decided to exhibit them, even though I was aware of their imperfections, my lack of technical knowledge, and the difficulties I had in always rendering what I wanted on the canvas. It was an act of daring, certainly, but also a great need. So I gathered together those pictures which represented me particularly well at that period. They were all figures – and chiefly faces – of people I had painted from my imagination, without there being any model. They possessed the characteristics of the self-taught, but from them sprang the features of my own disposition of soul, of my own general thinking about issues. These were apparent most of all in the eyes of the faces, which manifested a variety of human emotions.

I took my works to a small exhibition hall, and waited. I waited in hope. Hope for recognition of the work, for the confirmation of my talent, for a success in the world of art. The days passed, the exhibition drew towards its close – and hope began to falter. I foresaw failure. But, entirely unexpectedly, a review appeared in some newspaper. One of the best and most widely known art critics had visited the exhibition and had written very favourably about my works. Although she mentioned the element of the self-taught – which was glaringly obvious – she nevertheless gave emphasis to the workings of the soul which showed themselves through the faces, and she said, moreover, that these conveyed a message, they taught something. My hope had been fulfilled, and I would say that the fulfilment exceeded my expectations. When I read this account, my eyes filled with tears of emotion and I said to myself: "Now my life's purpose has been fulfilled. I am complete, it doesn't matter if I live any longer." I spoke to a lot of acquaintances about this review, and I constantly read it and re-read it. On the third day, my enthusiasm had begun to be moderated. Since my hope had become reality, new ideas began to overwhelm me. And then I remembered the words of the proverb: "Every miracle takes three days, and the biggest, four". The fourth day came, and with it all the magic came to an end. And then I said other things to myself: "And so what? What difference does it make to me if some noted critic has written what she has written? Now what happens from this point on? Is this the meaning of life – for someone to recognise something of yours? And then what?"

I was now in a void. I had nothing to hope for. But how was I to live without hope? What was I waiting for? But, even if I was waiting for something, and this became my new objective, might it not end up again in the same way? With a cycle being completed, with a success coming – if it came, of course – and then the void again. No answer came to my questions, and I no longer knew whether man should hope or not. Because what meaning does it have for him to pursue something for his whole life, and, when it comes – if it comes, naturally – to have to pursue something else? If a childhood dream, such as my success in the field of painting, didn't bring about a stability in happiness, what could bring about its stabilisation?

All this happened in January 1980, and I met the Master in June of that year. In the six months that intervened, I hadn't found anything else to build a vision upon, from which to acquire a new hope. Of course, as the mother of three children, I always hoped for the best for them, and as a wife, I wanted to live together harmoniously with my husband. But I had wanted these things for many years already, and they didn't constitute anything new, a new objective, a new expectation which was going to enchant me. And so I was not expecting anything special, but, deep down, I was always waiting for something, as, in any case, everybody does. What would this 'something' be? The answer came, of course, through the presence of the Master, who guided me to seek everything only from the higher self.

I have told this story because it was a turning-point in my life: a turning-point not so much for my painting, but above all for the change in my attitude on the subject of hopes. Of course, I didn't find out at that time what in the end ought to happen – should man hope, or shouldn't he? Neither the one nor the other seemed to me right. And I waited in a state of suspense, for the truth to reveal itself of its own accord. It came from heaven, as they say. That is to say, it came from my own self, the one that knows, which I found within myself with the help of the Master.

Discussions on the subject of hopes between the Master and the disciples have always been, without exception, stormy. A disciple comes and tells him of a hope that he has, and he starts to shout: "Oh, so then: you have hopes, you don't believe!" Somebody else comes along, bringing an idea which, he says, he hopes to put into practice. More shouting: "And why do you stop at plans and hopes? Why don't you put into action what you are saying?" At other times, another disciple makes his appearance; it seems from what he says that he is expecting something from his partner: then there is a fresh onslaught: "You're waiting for something. All you do is wait and wish. But from whom? When will you disciples understand that you mustn't wait for anything from anybody or anything. It is only God who gives everything; it is only to Him that you should address yourself. What can another human being give you that will bring you completeness?"

Disciples who are beginners are bewildered by this approach of the Master. "But how can I not expect something?" they often say. "Shouldn't the other person give us something, shouldn't they respond to our needs? If I don't hope for something, I see no meaning in life." It is impossible for this approach to hopes to change, if there aren't first many disillusionments, if the vanity of expectations is not proved to each individual. But, until that change comes, the Master continues to break down errors and dreams. "Don't wait for something – be it."

When I heard these words for the first time, I thought them completely absurd. How could I 'be' whatever it is I want? If I'm expecting a gift and nobody gives me it, am I able to become that gift? If, again, I hope to stir somebody's interest and that person continues to be indifferent, must I become his interest? This is unintelligible and unrealistic – for sure, I thought. Nobody can become a new dress, a professional success, a circle of friends. A human being is a human being, he's not the universe. "And yet he is", says the Master. "A human being encloses inside himself the whole of the universe. If he understands who his self really is, he will not hope for anything, because, quite simply, he will be everything."

At this point the conversation stopped, because when disciples are unable to grasp certain concepts, the Master doesn't insist. And, naturally, when a new current of hopes came, the disputes started again. The disciples hoped, wanted, expected, and he told them to believe, to act, to become themselves what they desired.

I can remember some very impressive lessons given to us by the Master at that time, to persuade us that man can be everything, and so not want anything. At such moments I couldn't contain myself and I would say to him: "Master, if some outsider heard what we're saying and doing now, he would have us locked up in a madhouse, no doubt about it." "Do you think so, Mrs Klairi?" he would reply, laughing. "Of course, Master. How can it not be thought crazy when you ask us if we want a cake, for example, and then you add that there's no reason for us to want it, because, quite simply, we are ourselves that cake. Things like that have sent plenty of people to psychiatric clinics. Don't you agree?" "I agree, but that doesn't mean that something that can't be explained by acquired knowledge is mad or impossible." And then he would go on with the lesson.

He would say, for example, to a disciple: "You tell me that you have a great longing for a certain girl. You like her, you'd like to have a relationship with her, but that's impossible because she's going to be engaged to someone else. You continue to hope, and you suffer. Do you know why you want her? Because you haven't seen that the girl is yourself, she is another aspect of you. If you see that, you won't want her any more; you will become her."

"And in what way is she myself? I don't understand. She's a girl and I'm a man. She has her own body, her own thoughts and emotions. And I have mine. How are we one? Anyway, don't you say yourself that sexual love helps in evolution?"

"Yes, that's exactly what I want to say to you. Your love for this girl will help you to evolve. But it isn't necessary for this to happen by way of a relationship, since, in any event, there's no question of anything of the kind. Consequently, love will bring the completeness which you want, that is, absolute union with the girl, if you work to become one with her, in soul and spirit. Then you will experience true love."

"But in that way I will be deprived of real contact, the pleasure of her presence with me."

"This contact is not real, it's only apparent, even if it seems to be the opposite. And it's only apparent because it involves the relations of the form and the personality of two people, and not their union deep down, which is experienced within and is not affected by time, distance, and individual manifestations. Anyway, forms change, and something which you like in a woman today may become different, and you may not like it some years later. Whereas the essence, the entity, remains unimpaired and, when you are in union with it, you won't be affected by any changes, since these do not exist in the essence."

"Oh, well, Master – all this that you are telling me seems to me a little bit like double-Dutch, but I'm tired of my vain hope, tell me what to do, in case this situation can change."

"It's simple, very simple. You must embrace this girl whom you like, just like everything else that you desire, in your soul, you must think that she is passing within you, and that you are inside her entity. You feel devotion, you live love inside yourself. You are completely united with her, and so you cease to want anything from her, not even her simple presence. Why should you want it, since you have become one? It's as if you want, let's say, your hand. But that's not what you want, because it's already a part of your self. Isn't that so?"

"So it seems, as you say; at least, I understand it intellectually. But there are needs, desires, emotions. I don't know if I can ignore them. Have I to stop experiencing love with a woman, even when this is attainable?"

"No, you will experience sexual love with a woman, as always – when, of course, there are no obstacles to this. Nor do you need to ignore anything; you simply have to become one with everything. You see a desire flaring up within you and you say immediately: 'myself and the desire'. This way of looking at it sets you over against the desire, it separates you from it. If, however, you say: 'I am the desire', then you will be one with it. But because you will also be one with the opposite – that is, with non-desire – you will find the balance, you won't sometimes want the one thing and sometimes the other, you will be both at the same time, living that which comes at every moment."

Normally the discussions about desires and hopes stopped at this point with the Master urging that the relevant meditations should take place, to bring about the consolidation of the concepts. All this teaching passed into our consciousness, but it was not easily integrated. Every so often new hopes came about new ideas which crossed our minds. Ideas which might not concern only a personal need, but could be even hopes for the spread of the work done at the Society. The Master would then say that the disciple should have visions and not hopes. Because a vision is a pure, powerful projection of an idea about the work, and not an emotional relation with it. He advised us to envision and believe that the whole of humanity is evolved spiritually and that there is love and unity among men; not to restrict ourselves only to hope, which conceals within it doubt, fears, and insecurities.

I had been a disciple for nearly a year now, and I hadn't yet reached the point of being able to bring about union with something in a complete way. Of course, certain very important transitions had taken place and had revealed to me in sensational ways that all things are, deep down, one. However, these revelations had come of their own accord, from the direction of the inner consciousness, which was goading me to pass on to substantial union. But I had not become anything by my own will, by my participating in the work of the higher consciousness, the inner self. Something would come unexpectedly, directly from another level of my self and would bring me a realisation, which, however, would be lost, since I didn't know how to make use of it.

One day, without my seeking any specific result, I brought to mind, when I was meditating, a plant which I had in the house. To begin with, I studied it simply, observing in thought its shape, its form, its roots. However, little by little I began to gain more interest in it, to feel a current of love. I allowed this current to emerge from me and embrace the plant, to penetrate the whole of it from the root to its sensitive little leaves. But as soon as this force of the soul went to the plant, I felt at once that I was no longer my familiar self, but that I was also its self, unknown to me. And suddenly the plant was no longer unknown to me, I was myself it, the two of us had become a greater united entity.

I remained for a long time in the same state, in order to get to know every particular of this new part of my ego. I experienced every energy which passed through it, I became one with its sap, its branches, its leaves. And while I was in an ecstasy within this existence, suddenly a noise was heard in the street, a load noise. Then a shudder passed through me, and I experienced this as a plant, not as a human being. It was if I – the plant – was shuddering all over, and my leaves contracted as if they had been hurt. When the noise stopped, the previous calm returned, and I decided to complete the meditation. What I had experienced was more than enough – particularly the experience of the vibration which came from the noise. Because I knew that plants are very sensitive to currents of energy, but, of course, I had never before experienced their sensitivity. I was astounded!

The same evening I told the Master what had happened, and he did something which took me by surprise. He seized my hand and kissed it, in the way that you do to a much revered figure, saying that he had a great reverence for me. I didn't fully understand what he meant, but gradually I saw that what he expressed at that moment was a reverence for the ontological field to which I'd given expression, the field of absolute union, where all is one. And precisely because this field is not personal, I didn't have at that time any personal satisfaction. See everything as it is, because, quite simply, that's how things are.

Of course, a single isolated conscious union is a mere trace element compared with the total union with all things which the Master teaches us. In the years which I have spent with him, it has been confirmed for me that the Master means union, because only if there is union, is there consciousness and knowledge and love. We are all taught union in a variety of ways. The Master is united; about that fact I no longer have any doubt. But to begin with, I sought to discover through specific actions if he truly is. Because with the proofs, the doubts left me and my belief in the teaching which I was receiving grew – a teaching which was delivering me from disappointments and hopes, and leading me to fullness.

At the beginning, I was at a loss whenever something happened which proved this function of the Master. One day, as I was going down the veranda stairs to go into the Society's garden, I saw the Master was meditating and turned back in order not to bother him. His voice interrupted me: "Come on, Mrs Klairi", he told me. And when I sat down next to him, he added: "Did you think that I didn't know that you'd come?" I was so taken aback that I didn't ask how he had realised this, because he had his eyes closed and I had made no noise. It is, of course, self-evident that the Master's union with his disciples enables him to perceive the currents which they emit and to know if they are near him, and if they have a problem or if they are well.

Often, at a time when I was going through severe fluctuations, the Master would phone me and ask how things were, whenever I was feeling bad. At other times, again, he would ask: "Have you got a headache?" I would say 'yes', because in fact I did have a headache. And when one day I asked him how he knew this, he told me that he too experienced my pain in his own head.

These things, and many others, happened constantly. I saw, for example, some symbol in my meditation and he, without my having told him anything about it, would analyse the symbol for me the next day. And I would say in amazement: "But, Master, that also came to me in meditation." Little by little I came to believe in the union which the Master experiences with everything, but always within human limitations. Because he often asks a disciple what he's thinking, what conversation took place on a particular subject, which members have come to the Society, and so on. When at the beginning I heard him ask such questions, I was puzzled. I couldn't connect these two opposing manifestations of him – that he sometimes knew and sometimes asked. I gradually came to understand that union is in a spiritual and energy field, but it is not necessary for it also to be in the natural field. He doesn't need to know, that is, the specific actions, because what is much more important is the inner processes, the currents which flood a person and make the corresponding actions a reality. The Master doesn't read the mind; he simply unites himself with the positive or negative current of thoughts and through this union can also supply the specific answer, if needed.

The teaching of union is always given in various ways and by innumerable methods. If the Master teaches the transubstantiation of hope into faith, it is because hope is only the desire for something and not conscious union with it. If he speaks of the transformation of desire into love, it is also because desire does not bring completeness, it simply leads man to work for the acquisition of completeness.

I once meditated on the theme 'Existence without Hope', and I saw that such a state can mean two exactly opposite things. For a human being not to have hope means that he is in despair. But for the inner man, for the entity within him, it means absolute completeness, union with everything, and, so, no need or hope for anything. As the Master says: "A person who is united does not hope, does not want anything; he is everything. And he lives the eternal miracle, which has no end or beginning!"

PERSONALITY - ENTITY

Great confusion reigned in my mind from the very first days of my discipleship over the matter of personality, and that confusion lasted for a long time. The Master had said, of course, that all of us disciples must develop our personality and not break it down, but these words didn't correspond to the events which were going on in that first year at the Society. I heard some things at one moment, and different things at another. I understood some things, the disciples said other things, and we all did different things.

As I was born and bred in that class of society which attaches particular importance to the 'person', I was unable to link what I had learnt there with what I was learning, or at least thought I was learning, with the Master. The value of personality is apparent in all those people who admire it whenever that is possible, and condemn it whenever it doesn't manifest itself or manifests itself in a way which is annoying and oppressive. Things were very clear-cut in society, but at the Servers' Society, at that time, they hadn't been cleared up at all.

I remember that one day my son, who was 17 at the time, had come to the Society with me, and spoke abruptly to some new member, so that there was a small misunderstanding. An older disciple then took me aside in the office and recommended that I shouldn't allow him to adopt such an attitude. I replied that my son had to learn how to express his personality, because he was still very young. He looked at me as though he didn't know what I was saying, and couldn't understand how I dared to speak about the needs of the personality. But because he too had heard the Master say that we must all learn to express ourselves, he said nothing against this need, but shifted his ground by saying: "But we can't let your son create problems, because he has to go through some cycles of experience in the field of personality". I was so confused about this matter that I made no reply. In any event, my son was not yet at that time a disciple of the Master. When he had asked to become one, the Master had told him that he was too young and should first serve an apprenticeship with his father, for at least a year. I found, then, the attitude of the older disciple towards my son very demanding, since he hadn't received any instructions from the Master. But I said nothing, because I had arrived at the point where I preferred not to speak rather than to hear that I was making mistakes because of my personality.

But it was not only the disciples who made things difficult. Often, the Master himself confused me by what he said. Once two disciples had quarrelled, and when they reported it to the Master, he said: "I see a lot of personality here". But another day he shouted at someone: "Why don't you express your personality, what are you afraid of?" What confused me even more was his attitude towards an elderly lady, a disciple with very discreet manners, polite, and soft-spoken. He said to her often, and with considerable irony: "Be careful not to lose your social masks; they're very important, you see". These and many other things brought me to an impasse. The strong personality, the weak, and the false – all were mistakes. Where was the right one to be found?

The problem wasn't mine only: no disciple had a clear opinion on this matter. And so we frequently asked the Master what sort of personality he had. He would answer in the familiar way by using contrasts. Sometimes he would say that he didn't have a personality, and sometimes that he is all the personalities of human beings. Naturally, he meant that as a separate person he did not have an individual ego which he wished to project, but as an inner field of consciousness of a Master he was united with all the aspects of human personalities. But at that time I was unable to understand this double nature – individuality which contains an overall consciousness. And so I remained in ignorance, thinking that the Master had a mania for speaking in oracles, just to make life difficult for us.

I did him an injustice, of course, because he was always analysing for us the importance of personality. He used to say: "The personality derives its light from elsewhere, like the moon. This is the reason that it's also referred to as the moon, which is symbolised by 18 in numerology. The light-giver of the moon is the sun, of course, and of the personality it is the higher self, the spirit within man. If we look only at the moon, which fascinates us with its constant changes, then we forget the source of its light. If we are distracted by aspects and phases, I would say, of the personality, we forget its inner giver, the spirit. But when we forget the spirit, we also forget our inner self. That is why I tell you to turn to within yourselves, and not to attach so much importance to appearances."

When I heard numerology mentioned, I hurried to my beloved reference books, but, I must admit, I didn't receive much illumination from them. It seems that the interpreters of the number 18 themselves are unable, or so I thought at the time, to give an account of the matter of personality precisely as it is. It is stated, of course, that 18 symbolises the material world, where the elaboration of the individual ego begins, but it is also stated that the soul is delivered only when it transcends the needs of this world. Thus, personality, which is an expression of form, seemed to me to be like a compulsive condition, since the soul wants to be delivered from it.

When I asked the Master, he replied:

"It isn't exactly like that. The soul needs the personality; it is, in a certain way, its tool. Through it, its energies and powers are expressed, so that man can see them and come to know them. As I've said before, we shouldn't reject the personality, but accept it; we should give it what it needs, we should develop it with love and understanding, as we do in the case of a child."

"Why then, Master, does it create so many problems for us? Why does it mislead us into endless expressions which are an error?"

"Because you are not doing as I said. That is, you don't see it as an immature part of your self, but you regard it as your chief characteristic. And it remains without control and governs you with its needs like a spoilt, unruly child."

I began to realise that the problem of man is that he doesn't know – or knows to only a very small extent – what powers he has within him. And since he doesn't know them, it is natural that he is left at the mercy of his personal needs and weaknesses. So I went on working with this knowledge, which would make me the handler of my personality, the immature part of myself. And while I was coming close to accepting its immaturity, the Master spoilt things for me again by saying one day that the personality conceals great wisdom deep within it. How was I now to connect these two opposites – that is, the wisdom and the childishness of the personality? Is there on this planet even one wise child? And so it was back to the beginning again, new sorting out of ideas, new mental processes, fresh doubts. So where then is its wisdom concealed, without being apparent? "And yet it is there, concealed", the Master says. "The personality is a great field of consciousness within the entity. This field has an important mission: to express all ideas, all situations, emotions, powers, and weaknesses. And all these should be expressed, because they are all aspects of the entity."

The Master never prohibited us from expressing our self. On the contrary, he would tell us to let our thoughts roam freely, our emotions and needs be expressed. Because if we prevent their externalisation, we shall not learn who we are. Of course, this freedom must be confined within reasonable and commonly accepted limits, and must follow the moral rules. In parallel with externalisation, he would bring in immediately the other position – that is, the restraint of freedom. When a disciple made a mistake, he would never leave him in error. Thus it was almost certain that the expression of personality would result in an unpleasant rebuke. And, of course, many disciples preferred not to show who they were, because they knew what awaited them if what they showed was not the right thing. But isn't perhaps the fear of expressing yourself again a negative manifestation of the personality? And, of course, the Master saw that as well. And so there was no way of escaping the thrust of his taking you apart, whether you expressed yourself or kept quiet, the same thing always happened.

There were innumerable episodes, and all had to do with the personality of the disciples. For example, there was a knock at the door and a disciple entered the room, to be greeted by the Master with these words:

"Ah! So you finally decided to knock. I could see your shadow from the window for five whole minutes. Why did you have to think so much about it since you want to see me? When will you gain confidence in yourself?" After a short interval, there was again a knock at the door – a loud one. The Master said his usual "Yes..." and as soon as the next disciple made his appearance, there was fresh shouting: "What sort of manners are these? Is that a way to knock at doors? Have you no respect for others?" The two sat down on their chairs like whipped dogs to wait for what was to follow. And I wondered "Why is he concerning himself now with such details? He should let them sit down first, because if he puts them down like that, they won't say a word."

But the Master maintained that we should give emphasis to detail, because it is from this that character, and the inner disposition, shows. The matter of detail caused me many inhibitions. I wanted to be perfect; I didn't like mistakes to be revealed through a word, a movement, an action on my part. I remember, at the time when the Master had entrusted me with doing the shopping for the Society, that the moment came for me to buy some coffee cups. Since at that time I assigned a very special place to the Master, I bought for him a more finished cup. This choice gave rise to a lot of irony, whose purpose was to break down the astral which I had with him, the special status which I assigned to his person. He used to say to me: "You see, the Master is something different from all the others. He can't have the same cup as they do... ." The disciples when they heard this for the first time, made fun of me, but immediately he struck them down as well: "Ah, you laugh, do you? You, of course, have no attachment to the Master. Isn't that so?"

All this made me angry or cast me down into despair. I began to be careful about every single thing that I did.

What colour blouse should I wear? Which chair should I sit on? Should I put my right leg over my left, or vice versa? Should I put the light on, or should I leave it off? Who should I speak to first, to a male or a female disciple? Because it was through such insignificant details that the Master saw and revealed to us the unconscious, our terrible enemy. He explained that everything symbolised something, and while he taught us its symbolisms, he interpreted at the same time the symbols which were connected with our personal issues. Thus, whereas we were enthralled by the knowledge we were receiving, at the same time we were disillusioned over the painful revelations of our self.

Years passed, and still I wondered what to do with this personality. Was I to express it, to suppress it, to reject it, to accept it, to obey it, to refuse it, which of these things was the disciple to do? "You are to make use of it", the Master would say. "And how is use made of something so strong and immature?" "By maturing it and using its strength. Because this strength becomes weakness when it is not directed by the true power within man."

At this point in the conversation, things took another turn: we left behind the personality and moved on to the Entity. Or, rather, we attempted to move on to the Entity, that elusive field. The Master says: "The Entity is the power, the essence, the pure nature within everyone and in everything. The disciple must seek after its power and the purity of its nature. The more he seeks it, the more it will be revealed within him, and the disciple begins to experience union with his nature. Union helps him to recognise fields and sub-fields of the Entity within his personality and to handle them as parts of himself. This brings about a change of the personality." "Is it, then, an ontological personality?" "Better that you should not use such terms. It is more correct to say that it is a personality which expresses pure power, and not some of its small, debased fields. Personality is itself the Entity, it is the aspect of the Entity which contains its essence. If this is recognised, then there will be no problem."

I began to watch the Master, to see whether he expressed the pure power and in what way he did it. What I saw immediately was that the ways varied, depending on the needs of the disciples or of events and situations, as I have said. But I wanted to see the ontological power in various external manifestations, its expression through the person of the Master.

Having learnt from human relations to colour the internal stance of each person chiefly from the way in which he showed himself, I had the greatest difficulty in overcoming this barrier. I saw the Master show anger, for example, and I immediately thought that he was angry – that he also was the slave of a weakness. I saw him being indifferent, not answering some questions, and I thought that he was concerned with his own problems. Faced with each new expression of this kind, I began to meditate on what was hidden behind this and why it manifested itself in this way.

Gradually I saw that the Master was playing with the various aspects which he was projecting. And he was able to play with them precisely because he was above them. And then his words – that life is a game – which had angered me so much in the past, came to my mind. People don't play with life, because we become trapped in its own games and we become its pawns. But the consciousness within us, our higher nature, guides the game like a perfect chess-player. It moves our aspects, sets them in conflict with one another, mixes them up, and re-arranges them in innumerable combinations. Like the black and white pawns in chess, the small powers within us fight between themselves until the end of the game. But above all these is the player, his power and knowledge which directs the flows.

The Master, in union with the power within him, plays all the roles of the opposing forces, in order to maintain balance. He is sure of his inner self and has a knowledge of its various manifestations. I would say that the Master is a man of many faces; he acts all the characters but is not governed by any of them. Because he always remains impersonal, which means that he is detached from personal issues and individual needs. The same thing has been confirmed to me in the meditation which I did on power; that this is entirely spontaneous and handles all the forces, to project many forms. But knowledge of this power at one level of consciousness is one thing and seeing that this can also be expressed by another person is another. As I saw that the Master, although a man, expresses the power of the entity, I began to wish to be like him more and more. And then the Master said that this is a matter of decision. If someone decides to sacrifice his small desires and to unite himself to the one and only great will of God, then he can become one with the Master within him. A condition of deliverance is that this sacrifice is made over the years, as the disciple ceases to be concerned with his self and concerns himself only with the problems of others.

All the study which I carried out on the entity of the Master led me to the conclusion to which many other observations had also led me. I saw, simply, that everything was leading to one position, the position of the decision on union with the higher self. It is on this that the disciple must ground himself.

When disciples ask the Master when this change can finally happen, he replies: "Now. This very moment. It's a matter of making up your mind. Do it now, at once. Don't stay in a position of weakness and of the needs of the personality, but pass on to your ontological power. It's a matter of decision, and you can take this whenever you wish. Everything else then comes of its own accord. The disciple abandons himself in faith to his inner self, and everything follows its path without any difficulty."

THE GIVER

There were many things which fascinated me when I met my husband: the eight languages which he spoke, his highly developed intelligence, his knowledge of many varied subjects.

And there were two subjects which entranced me when he spoke about them, as if an unintelligible need was drawing me to learn as much as I could to capture their meanings. Although they were complete opposites of one another, nevertheless they both found the same resonance within me. I used to sit and listen to him talking, asking many questions in between, so that no detail of his vivid descriptions escaped me.

The first subject, about which he spoke to me on the very first day of our acquaintance, was the incredible experiences which he had had during his four years of life in India. His work in that country had involved many trips to isolated villages where people live with many strange beliefs about the unknown powers which circulate among us as negative spirits or which manifest themselves as magic or as transformations of human beings into animals, and much else besides. I sucked in every word he spoke, in order to digest its meaning. He passed on to me stories he had heard about magicians who could cure all illnesses, about people who had been possessed by evil spirits, about mysterious noises heard in the night. Although very often I didn't believe these stories and considered them fantasies of uneducated Indians who, as I knew, lived in various regions far removed from civilisation, I couldn't disprove them either. In order for them to believe in such phenomena, even if they exaggerated them by means of their imagination, there had to be something behind them. But what was it that was behind them?

The second subject of our conversation was entirely different. It concerned astronomy, in which my husband had had a great interest since childhood, and had studied a great many works of science on the subject. There was, moreover, a time, later, when he had bought a telescope and made his own observations, teaching our children how to study the moon and the stars. I had also had an interest in astronomy since I was a child. I can remember how much I liked to hear an uncle of mine explain to me about the different constellations, and how excited I was at school by the cosmography lesson. And so the much fuller knowledge of my husband on this subject held me transfixed in his company, listening to him talk about the galaxies, about the motion of suns, their birth and disappearance, and all the many other details which he had read. All this magic of creation prompted me to search again for what was hidden behind its countless manifestations.

These two completely different subjects had for me a common characteristic: mystery – the often inconceivable phenomenon, the unknown element in life. I asked myself how it was possible for a magus, for example, to perform cures, and how it was possible for a sun suddenly to be born in space. I tried to find out what there was beyond these phenomena, because I was unable to imagine how they could come about in this way on their own. There was something there, and I didn't know what it was and where it was to be found.

As life rolled on and gave us many cares about the family which we had had, these conversations became rarer. We were more taken up with immediate everyday problems. But always nesting within me was this quest for that unknown something which is the motive force of the universe and of man. I remember that one day, while I was cooking and my husband was coming in and out of the kitchen, I said to him, entirely unexpectedly: "And yet, you know, there must be something there." Surprised, he asked me what I was talking about, what I was referring to, because there had been no previous conversation. "Look, I'm saying that life can't be what it seems. I can't accept that we are born in order to grow up, to have children, and then to die. That seems to me without significance, without meaning. There must be something else, something that we don't know about. A power... I don't know what." "You must be right", he replied, "but – what am I to say – I don't know either."

Years passed without any answer. But there was faith within me, a belief in the existence of the unknown power which brings birth and death, which gives all things, whatever these are. I wasn't able to conceive of anything else; I did not understand. I didn't want to give a form to the power in some being, because then I would be limiting it. In any event, I didn't devote much time to these questionings, they simply sprang up of their own accord at unexpected moments, when something was very interesting or strange, or, on the contrary, when everything became monotonous and boring. It was then that the need awoke to search for something else.

And then the time came when I met the Master and put to him the same question: what is the power which is concealed behind the phenomena of life? His answer was monosyllabic. "God", he told me. "Big deal!" I thought at the time. "Thank you very much for this new information. We all know that we call this power God. But what is it?" In a few days, I asked him the second question: "And what is God?" The Master said: "God is God. He isn't anything else." "Oh, I see", I thought again. "It's a great philosophy, is this! God is God, he says. And a cigarette is, of course, a cigarette. I'm afraid this Master whom I've gone and found knows no more than I do. I've been taken in again."

Finally, I heard the last incredible thing, which bowled me over even more than the ones before. Arriving a little late for a lesson of the Master's, I entered the room at the moment he was saying: "And so, in this sense, that is, that God is everything, we could also say that God is also the cigarette which we smoke." "That's crazy!" I said to myself. "I thought of that as sarcasm, and now he's saying it as though it's true. Whoever heard of such a thing? God is a cigarette! I'll smoke Him, and then He won't exist any more."

Although I laughed ironically to myself about all this, I wasn't able to give up my discipleship. Because although, of course, the Master had not given me the answer which I had been looking for for years, he gave me a number of other important answers. And I certainly needed these; I had to learn whatever he knew how to teach me. In any case, I wasn't at all interested at that time in religions and theology; what interested me, apart from personal issues, was the matter of the unknown power which generates existence, which made me think, which ever since I was a child I had felt all around me, without ever knowing what it was. "So", I thought, "I'll leave everyone to look upon God in whatever way he wishes, and let's see if I can understand who or what it is that gives life. Because something must certainly give it, and this something is not man, nor is it any other limited creature. It is, it must be, unbounded."

All these ideas about the unknown power made it very difficult for me to understand that the Master was talking about this all the time, from the first moment that I met him, and that he was talking about it all the time in all the lessons which he gave. The concept of God is exactly the same as the power which I had been looking for; He is exactly this unknown and all-powerful giver I had been searching for. And in order that I – and all the disciples – should find Him, the Master told us that God is everywhere present. In order to lend particular emphasis to His presence everywhere, he had quoted the unlikely example of the cigarette. In later lessons, I heard him speaking about the Entity, about the higher self, about overall existence, universal consciousness, the supraconscious state, the void of which Buddha speaks – and all those things which in the end he called God. This is the one and only field which he was always talking about, on whatever subject he was speaking.

My first efforts to realise the presence of God everywhere were very limited. I saw Him only in those things which I considered beautiful, in high ideals, in great ideas. I was unable to imagine His presence in a worm, an illness, or in anything else which seemed to me 'lower'. And so God was for me at that time something a great way off, which, of course, was giving me strength, was giving me life, but which I was never able to get near. The Master would repeat the words of the Bible and of the sacred books of other religions – that God is everywhere present and fills everything, and so is also within us. "But if He is within me, why can't I understand and conceive of His presence?" "God is not understood or conceived of; He is only revealed", the Master would say. "And what must man do? Must he sit around and wait for this revelation? And if it never comes?" "No, he doesn't wait. He works constantly for it to come whenever it is to come." "And what work does he do?" "He simply begins to manifest a very little, what he is able to each time, of the sublime qualities of God: love, strength, knowledge. And the more he manifests these towards everybody and everything, the more his work leads him towards revelation."

In these words I saw that the Master was talking again about service and about the sacrificing of the individual ego. And, naturally, when I refused to serve, I passed into a state of opposition, even to this unknown power which is everywhere. And I used to say to the Master: "You say that God is the sole giver of all things. And so it is He who has given problems to human beings. So why should I now help them to overcome them? Let Him help them." "He helps everybody and everything and certainly He will find the solution to the problems you speak of, if that solution is going to help people. The issue lies elsewhere – whether you will perform service, so that the power of God within you is revealed."

At other times, again, I didn't understand at all why the all-powerful giver gives illnesses and misfortunes. Everything could be simple, easy, beautiful. What is the reason for all these problems? "God does not give the problems in the way that you imagine", the Master would reply. "He gives strength, knowledge, love, but man, who doesn't know what he is receiving, reverses it all by his ignorance". "So why doesn't God also give him a knowledge of what he is receiving? Is there a reason for man having so much ignorance?" "But He does do that, Mrs Klairi. Ignorance is the stimulus for knowledge, because only if knowledge is acquired through experiences, does it have a true value, is it true consciousness."

Little by little, as time passed, I began to see that the power which I had been looking for is everywhere. I had read somewhere that the saints, when they were ill, glorified God for this gift that He had given them, their illness itself. This is difficult as a concept, and much more difficult to put into practice. As it is also difficult for man to accept that financial difficulties, a family problem, social upheaval are gifts which are given to him for his own good. We want everything as we think it ought to be, but, at the same time, we don't do what we should for these things. "Bring about God within yourselves", the Master says. "Give expression to the power which you possess, so that the positive result will come."

Work and again work. Years of intensive discipleship, for some feature of this power to be projected. And in the meantime, countless ups and downs and backslidings into childish manifestations. "Master", one disciple used to say, "why doesn't God give me a good job, when I ask this of Him continually?" "You ask for it, but do you do what you should for the job to be found? Do you express the power and the will for this? Do you believe that it will be found, or do you simply wait and hope?" Another disciple, again, asked: "But why am I ill so often? Why does God give me so many illnesses?" "God gives you strength and health, but you keep them inside yourself, you don't express them, you don't do any creative work. That's why you get ill."

Once, my husband told me a story about the attitude of people to God, when they refuse to accept that He is love and goodness. Then they turn against Him and He becomes their enemy. There was, he said, a madman, the madman of some village. As always happens, his fellow-villagers amused themselves with him whenever they had the opportunity. One day two friends went to find him so that they could have a little laugh. They saw him in his house, holding a rope and beating the air with it all around him. They asked him at once what he was doing, laughing in advance at his answer. What they heard went beyond all their expectations. The madman said: "I'm sure to catch Him somewhere. Isn't He present everywhere?" And he went on beating the air, in order to cause God pain, because he held Him responsible for his problems.

With whom did the madman have a grudge, and with whom do we have a grudge when we're not successful in something, or don't understand life? None other than our own higher self. We complain, we consider ourselves wronged, we behave like spoilt children who are constantly seeking gifts and toys from their parents and then cry when they won't let them have them and make them do their homework. God is the highest fatherhood and the highest motherhood of all beings. So how can this most sublime of all fields wrong its own children, when even ordinary parents do all that they can to be fair?

"Master, God cannot be grasped. How am I to believe in him?" a disciple asked. "You will believe in what you cannot grasp through what you can. Look at your body, look at the flower in the vase. Look at the stars in the sky, the sun, the moon. Look at the pebbles on the beach, listen to the birds singing. Observe your thoughts. All these things and countless others show the power of God. Why do you doubt?" The disciple fell silent, and went away to think, to meditate, to unite himself with God, who gives everything.

One day when I wanted to be convinced that God is what the Master says, the sole giver of all things, I decided to meditate. Exactly one month of discipleship had passed and all the answers which I had received through meditation were by way of symbols. As soon, then, as I had closed my eyes and relaxed, in order to go more deeply into the concept of the giver, a brilliant sun came as a vision. To begin with, I thought it had nothing to do with the subject that concerned me, but I soon realised that it had a direct relevance. Because the sun is the life-giver of the planets, and so through it I was able to go on to God as the giver. The sun which I saw had a human face and soon opened its mouth as if inviting me to go into it. I let happen what was to happen and felt that I was leaving my body and passing into the sphere of the sun. Then some force prompted me to go closer to its eyes and to look through these at the world around the sun. Next to me I saw some figures of saints and hierarchs.

I looked with the eyes of the sun and saw all the planets. Then the radiance, the light, the heat began to spread to the planets in constant currents of giving. I felt my heart expanding, loving the planets; I felt myself becoming the sun, wishing to give them all that they needed. And I felt my mind watching with ceaseless care every detail of them. I didn't keep anything for myself, I was radiating the whole of my being to my planets. And I was deluged with a happiness which seemed to generate melodious sounds, brilliant colours, beauty filled with calm. I now wanted nothing else. I had become the solar system.

I completed the meditation, which was the most important of any that I had performed so far. I had been given a first sense of giving, through a heavenly body. This giving must be inconceivable, if we consider that it supplies all the suns of the universe. For many hours I no longer wanted anything else.

When I reported this meditation to the Master, he replied that the disciple must at some time become a small sun. He must spread the energies of the soul around him as a brilliant radiance, must himself become the giver – at his own level, of course. But I said to him that the disciple is not God, since even the Master is not God. How then can he become a giver? He made the following analysis:

"The only giver is the Absolute, but within the Absolute there are fields and sub-fields of a differing breadth of consciousness. All these fields are recipients of the one field, but at the same time can also become givers to some inferior fields. The Master, for example, is a giver for his disciples, and the disciples become givers for the people who seek to learn something from them. In any event, the same thing happens in life: the father gives to the son, the big brother to the younger, and the younger to the one who is younger than he is. The giving in which you are being trained is precisely what happens every day in society. But the difference is that as you are trained in increasingly conscious functioning, in every act of giving which you perform, you should refer to the one giver, God, who is above all the other, smaller givers, since He supplies them all with the power which they need."

"As you were speaking, Master, an enormous machine with innumerable cogs of different sizes, all moved by the central cog, the biggest of all, came into my mind. If one of the smaller cogs stops, then a larger one will propel it forcefully into starting up again. If, however, this doesn't happen, then the cog breaks down and has to be replaced. It must be something like that with the power of God, which is diffused to the fields and sub-fields, so that they all operate in dependence on their range of consciousness."

"That is quite a good concept, but, naturally, it is some distance from the Absolute. Because the Absolute doesn't have a specific centre of power at some special point in the universe. The Absolute is Absolute everywhere alike. However, in order to help you, I would say that we can indeed see a small cog as a small field of consciousness which, when it doesn't enter into the flow of the power of life, needs a push in order to go ahead. Isn't this, anyway, what the Master does for the disciples? Doesn't he push them on the path of truth, 'pressuring' them, as the disciples say, so that they don't suffer pain from resistance to the flow of life?"

"You said before that the Absolute is the same everywhere. What do you mean by that?"

"The Absolute is present in all the fields, in the small and the great alike. But the fields do not have this knowledge; man can't, for example, conceive of the concept of the Absolute which exists within him, because he is enclosed within his limited human self. But man's difficulty doesn't change the fact that God is alike within everything, He is the essence which is not alloyed by forms. For this reason, in any event, there are those who have reached union with the Absolute, because it was there within them, as it is everywhere else."

"Master, this conversation has helped me a good deal.

I have begun to see what 'giver' means and to feel awe before the One Giver of everything. I shall begin to become a small giver myself, following the example of the Master, as it has been confirmed to me that he gives his soul for the disciples. Thank you, Master."

"It is God you should thank for all things. He gives everything. He is the sole Giver."

JUDGMENT AND DISCERNMENT

The disciple has the property of changing his decisions with great frequency, until, of course, he is firmly established in his position. Then things are different: he advances towards his goal, acknowledging the existence of probable obstacles which he will encounter, but without departing from the line which he has mapped out for himself or from the task which he wishes to perform. But until he arrives at this stability, great fluctuations occur. He decides upon something one day, and the next day the decision is different. He wants, or believes that he wants, to play his part in a common task, and then forgets this act of will, because he chooses to be shut up within himself. But he even frequently changes his decisions about his own self, because sometimes his personal desires lead him astray, and sometimes he follows the inclination of his soul.

These vacillations seem to be very normal for the first stages of a discipleship which has the broadening of the individual ego as its aim. But they are not as personal as they appear. On the contrary, they have a direct connection with the group unconscious, which serves to rein in the decision of the individual. The disciple who goes through severe crises in essence is being judged by his consciousness as to whether he is worthy to emerge from the group unconscious and to rise above it. The difficulty of this passage is great and occurs in cycles, depending on each occasion on the experiences and consolidation which have been acquired by each individual. And, naturally, the crises are more severe at the beginning of a discipleship, when there is not yet any consolidation. Of course, I would say that even in other stages of discipleship also there are similar crises, as one cycle of experiences closes and the next opens for further broadening of the consciousness. But then there are the previous experiences which help the disciple to react with knowledge; this is something which is entirely lacking in the beginning, and it is for this reason that he is vulnerable.

From the first day that I went to the Society and before I'd had time to understand a few things, I felt a climate of opposition surrounding me. Friends and acquaintances set out all together to save me – as they put it – from an impending disaster. Sometimes I had the feeling that as I was about to take a step on a new path which I had just found, the rest were stretching out their hands to pull me back, telling me I was heading directly for the cliff's edge. And, naturally, I was alarmed; I turned back to listen to them, lost my way, and then had to start over from the beginning again.

When I told my friends that I was attending lessons at a spiritual centre, I had to listen to many strange things. The first of these was: "Be careful! Because the people at such centres take drugs." Although I reassured them that nothing of the sort went on at our centre, nevertheless this gave rise to suspicions within me. How was I to know what the others did on the days when I wasn't there? I began to look suspiciously at the Master and the disciples, in case they showed symptoms of being drug addicts. And when I came close to believing that there was no such problem, someone would say to me: "You're still very new; that's why they hide from you. You'll see, in a little while they'll give you some too, and then it will be too late." New doubts, new investigations in order to be sure what went on at the Society.

Before I was well and truly convinced that nobody took drugs, and that precisely the opposite was true, given that the Master cured addicts by spiritual healing, a new charge was levelled. A friend approached me with an air of mystery and said to me: “Klairi, they'll make you change your religion. I know what I'm talking about. All of those people are of other religions, they belong to other denominations.” I explained to her, of course, that the teaching I was receiving was a philosophy which dealt with all the currents and brings them together for them to develop globally and for us to be united with God, but she insisted:

“No, no. These are pretexts. That's what they tell you, but you don't know what's hidden behind it.” I again began to have doubts. Was I going to end up a Muslim or a Buddhist?

There were similar very marked reactions from my environment when I decided to do something for others. Then, as if they knew of my intention, in some way which was inexplicable to me at that time, all my acquaintances rushed to undermine this decision. They put me in the dock and fired off their accusations against me, but in essence these were addressed against the spiritual work which I wanted to embrace. I was, they said, very naive, very weak, I believed in people I didn't know, I allowed myself to be exploited, I was becoming a laughing-stock – and a thousand other things. And as I was still far from sure about anything, I was frequently influenced by their doubting and, naturally, refused again to perform service.

I had just gone through an acute crisis of this kind when I decided for the first time to take up a more responsible position in the Society, as the Master had recommended to me. This position was very simple and absolutely natural, in the light of the objective circumstances. As I have already explained, the Master's disciples at that time were some young people, and I was the first mature woman. It went without saying that I should take up a role of a mother, who supervises, advises, and cares for the younger ones. This, then, was what the Master was calling upon me to do: to give my interest and love to the younger disciples. My first thoughts were: "To give? Why should I give, and what am I to give them? What are they expecting from me?" But when I saw their eyes looking at me, I began to regard them as my children, because, anyway, they were about the same age as my own children. Later, again, the idea of taking even the smallest responsibility for others wearied me.

It was then that the Master spoke to me about the role of a woman, of a mother in embracing people's needs and giving her love. I began to think again about the position which I should take up, and then, quite suddenly, I remembered something strange which had happened in the past at a time when it was totally unexpected. As I was sitting there, a image from the time when I was still young, a pure vision, came into my mind. I saw myself at a mature age, sitting in an armchair and talking to young people, who were waiting for me to talk to them, to smile at them, to fondle their heads. This memory, which showed the aptitude of my soul for being a true mother, broke down my resistances as it rose up from the past, and I agreed to take on a position of supervision in the Society.

As soon as I took this decision, it was as if the world turned upside-down. A friend of my children came that evening to the house and began to speak against the Master, although he had never met him. But he spoke about him from the stance that all Masters are cheats and charlatans. When the young man left, there was a conversation with my husband; although up to that day he had agreed that I should receive this teaching, he suddenly told me that I should cut down on the hours which I spent at the Society. This was entirely unexpected, because my husband had always shown a great understanding of my needs and had never been an obstacle to me. And finally, the next day, first thing in the morning, I was visited by a lady I knew who was aware of what my new concerns were, and who brought me a newspaper article which gave a critical account of the operations of certain suspect spiritual centres whose existence I hadn't even heard of.

All these sudden negative attitudes towards the teaching made me give way and begin to have doubts again.

When in the evening the Master saw my expression, he asked me what had happened. I told him of the events and the disturbance which they had created in me. He said that it was natural that all these things should find expression, because I had taken a positive decision on the previous day. He added, moreover, that the counter-field always acts in this way. Since I didn't understand what he meant, he gave me a first analysis of the unconscious.

"Within the unconscious of man, of the whole of humanity, there are two aspects, the positive and the negative, that is, the field and the counter-field. And, to make myself clearer, there is the inclination of the soul towards spirituality, on the one hand, and the need of the personality for appropriation and individualism, on the other. Whenever one or more individuals express one of these two fields of the unconscious, the opposite is immediately also activated, in an effort always to gain the upper hand. This happens in the same way with both aspects; that is, wherever unhappiness, for example, makes its appearance, some people make theirs to provide help. But the negative manifests itself much more strongly when someone wishes to express goodness, love, service. And this happens because, as we have said before, humanity is still polarised in the personality."

"As, therefore, you have taken the decision on a beginning of the expression of love and service, the opposite aspect – the refusal of service – through your own unconscious itself, has united with the unconscious of other people in order to deter you. This is how the fact that all these negative currents came so suddenly and unexpectedly is explained. Of course, since we're talking about a completely unconscious function, because nobody knows that he has within him the refusal of spirituality, the people who have spoken to you believed that everything they said to you is for your good, and not to prevent your work."

"But how, Master, did all of them know what was happening with me, because I hadn't said anything about my decision?"

"They didn't know, but they didn't need to know. As we've said, these things function unconsciously. As your position brought about a change in the vibration of the unconscious, which is, I repeat, common to all humanity, the change in it reverberated in the opposite unconscious, the need for spirituality not to be expressed."

"That's all very strange, Master, but now that I think about it, I remember what happened a few days ago with another disciple. He had decided to break off certain relationships with people who were distracting him from study, so that he was in danger of failing the year at university. He told me yesterday that he had only just left the Society, resolved to go home to study, when on the next corner he met by chance three of these friends, and went off with them again to make a night of it. Did the same thing happen there, Master - did the counter-field make its appearance there too?"

"Precisely. Only the meeting was not a matter of chance. It had been caused, unconsciously, of course, through the positive attitude of the disciple, which vibrated the negative one. That's why I tell you that nothing is random, simply unconscious. It is precisely there that the meaning of testing lies hidden. Whenever someone takes a decision, the opposite aspects are projected, to test and finally to see whether he is really ready to do what he wishes. In this way stability in the decision comes, and then the obstacles no longer have force."

By means of this conversation, I realised that I had to remain firm in my decision, so that the unconscious factors within me would be broken down and the resistances of others reduced. The importance of stability was confirmed for me the same evening, when I returned home. My husband, who was united in soul with me, asked forgiveness for his reaction in the morning, saying that he didn't understand what had happened to him. He repeated that he was in agreement with the work of the Society and with the task which I wished to perform. In the years which followed, I noticed that whenever I had to overcome new, conscious or unconscious opposition, someone issued me with a challenge, in order to show whether I was ready for the new responsibilities, for the new broadening which I wished to make.

Gradually, in the circle of my family and friends, the opposition stopped. Even those who do not identify with the work of the Society maintain a neutral attitude towards it. They no longer hinder me by their words or their actions. Of course, the unconscious always exists and manifests itself wherever there is access for it to do so. Forms of opposition always make their appearance in the world of the Society, whenever a disciple of the whole group has to make a new transition.

Everybody is attacked by the group or individual unconscious and by the derivations of the counter-field. These, as I have come to realise, are never going to stop. And that is in fact what always happened in the years that followed, and still continues to happen. When I was teaching new groups, I would often hear about the specific obstacles which our members met from their environment, from themselves, and from various external happenings. At the time when, for example, someone was getting ready to come to the lesson, friends would come to visit him and so he would stay at home. At other times, somebody would set out and on the way would lose his wallet, or wouldn't find a taxi, and would suddenly feel unwell. There were also more difficult cases, such as constant opposition of a spouse to the discipleship of his/

her partner, or unforeseen family problems which distracted the disciple from the teaching, and many other things. I carried out for new members the analyses which I had heard from the Master, adding the relevant examples from my experiences.

Sometimes people's charges and suspicions advanced to other levels. Some, moreover, came and asked me outright what was hidden behind the work of the Society. Others tried to find out which political party was supporting us, others maintained that for sure we were a 'finger' of some foreign government, while others looked for the hidden financial benefit we were receiving - which, they said, must have some connection with some multinational corporation. And, naturally, most people wanted at all costs to see us as a branch of an Eastern religion.

To everything that was said I gave the same answer: that the Society was set up as a result of the impulse of certain people to respond to the great needs of society. That we had no financial, political, or religious support from anyone at all, and that the only revenues that there were was the small contribution of the members to meet expenses. I stressed that apart from this income, which was absolutely necessary, any other form of service was carried out without selfish motives. My words gave rise to differing reactions: some believed me, others doubted, and still others were unable to accept that we work without being paid by anyone.

As the years passed, dealing with such thoughts seemed to me very simple; the opposition and doubts didn't bother me. However, once something happened which drove me wild. I considered that this had overstepped the limits. That day, I had left the Society earlier than usual, because I had a family obligation. The disciples who remained went to the Master's room, where he gave them a new pattern of meditation which would help them to pass to a deeper and more substantive consciousness. As soon as the meditation had ended and a discussion had started about the disciples' individual experiences, a loud sound of breaking glass was heard. The disciples rushed to see what had happened, and found the glass front door shattered and some stones thrown into the entrance. Somebody had thrown stones at the Society's door, and had then disappeared.

When I heard what had happened, I was incredibly angry with the unknown culprit. I thought that whatever he had against the Society, the teaching, and the disciples, he had no right to express so much aggressiveness. I told the Master that it was not permissible for him to stone us over a difference of views. But he replied: "Why are you so struck by this episode? Haven't we examples from the past where a spiritual task has been combated with great force, rage, and hatred? What has happened is nothing compared with other things that have happened. Very frequently spiritual people have even been put to death by the counter-field. Socrates was sentenced to death, the school of Pythagoras was burnt down by arson, Gandhi was assassinated. And, of course, the greatest Teacher of love, Jesus, was crucified."

I was not pleased by the words of the Master, nor was my anger diminished. On the contrary, added to this was now sadness over mankind, who murders its spiritual guides, or prevents them by any possible means from delivering the messages which they have to. The thought that a spiritual undertaking has to face so much opposition wearied me and disillusioned me.

"You shouldn't see only the negative element in such events", the Master said, in order to relieve me of my distress and to help me to understand yet another thing. "What is manifested by aggressiveness is not only negative. Often, or, rather, I would say, always, it also conceals the positive, as we have said so many times. The specific attitude of people in combating spirituality also hides their great need to come to know it, to be delivered through it. But because they haven't reached the point of believing in love, in selflessness, in service, they express their negation by provoking spiritual people into doing something to deliver them from their unbelief. They test, I would say, the power of the Spirit so that they can be totally convinced of its existence. And for them to be convinced, some people have to give them concrete proof, to sacrifice themselves, to be distressed, to suffer. This is why they attack, whereas deep down they would like to achieve union."

"Their attitude reminds me of the attitude of children, Master. When I worked in the infants' school, I noticed that when a child wished to play with another one who didn't take any notice of him, he would pinch him, hit him, or kick him in order to gain his attention, to make him take notice of him."

"But we have said, Mrs Klairi, that the weaknesses and needs of the personality are the children of our spiritual nature. Only, whereas in the example which you have given, the other child may have paid back the assaults, because he was also a child, in the case of the spiritual person, it isn't like that. Because in him there is maturity, love, and sacrifice. But what are you thinking now, to make you take on that expression?"

"It occurred to me that it's possible that somebody might attack you – the one who broke the glass, for example."

"No, don't think like that. That doesn't happen to all Masters. In any case, there are the disciples. If the disciples are alright and don't have gaps, then the Master, who is in essence, their consciousness, is not in danger. If you, for example, are completely stable in your position, then the negative field will not find a way in to attack the spiritual work, and so to try to injure the Master."

"But how can you say that? Jesus was crucified, even though he had the Apostles around him. We are nothing compared to them."

"The Apostles were very developed, dedicated to Christ and to God, but don't forget Judas; through him the Pharisees got to Jesus and crucified him. But wasn't the total sacrifice of the Lord to help all those who persecuted him? Didn't this act redeem people, didn't it make the martyrs, didn't it spread his teaching? You can find similar examples of self-sacrifice in other religions if you read their sacred texts. Naturally, all these are sublime examples which I've quoted to you so that you can see the behaviour of mankind towards spirituality. The Master, as I've told you many times, is not God, is not Christ, nor the founder of any religion. He is an ordinary man and his disciples are people who are simply expressing an inclination to find out the truth about themselves and to unite themselves with God. But since this simple function comes into conflict with the personality, certain negative reactions find expression."

"I understand what you're saying completely, Master. But the critical attitude of others still distresses me. Judgments without any foundation, which in the end cause psychological disturbance in me. What am I to do? Very well, I've managed so far, but the stone-throwing has brought back to me everything I've had to listen to and I'm in a sorry state."

"You will get over that if you arrive at the point of discerning what is hidden behind every condemnation. Discernment must be the goal of every disciple. You should not confine yourself only to appearances – to aggressiveness and to the negative judgments of others – but you should go more deeply into the unconscious part of their manifestations, to their need to be delivered from what is binding them. Consciousness, the inner Master, never resists the unconscious needs of man. Because conscious knows, it has the discernment to see into the depths of things. The more you unite yourself with your consciousness, the more you will remain at a distance from the judgments of others, because you will discern their deeply hidden need."

"And how is discernment developed?"

"By meditation and experience. And, of course, by the belief that behind every negative there is the positive."

"And when discernment is developed, what then?"

"Then no accusation is an accusation, but becomes an invitation to greater service. No condemnation is regarded as a condemnation, since there is the knowledge that this is in essence a cry for help. Then the disciple dedicates himself with his soul to the work of spirituality and all is well."

The Master's words calmed me, because, in any event, the episode which had upset me didn't occur in either the first or the second year of my discipleship. I had now become accustomed to many positive and negative things, and one more manifestation couldn't throw me for long. So I stopped bothering about the culprit who had done the damage and saw to it that the pane of glass in the door was replaced immediately. Although I had various suspicions about two or three individuals who may have had such aggressiveness, because they were unable to accept the teaching, nevertheless I didn't think it was so important to find who was to blame. What was of importance was what we disciples would do from now on to become real servers; to speak with faith and to have the discernment to see the truth in everything. This position was required of us and it was with this that I decided to concern myself, until it was well and truly established in my conscience and was expressed dynamically towards everyone.

And while I was working towards this aim, at the same time I was studying the human tendency towards judgments and accusations. I saw that this does not attack only spiritual centres, it does not confine itself to an unconscious resistance to the inner Master and those people who wish to give expression to a broader field of consciousness. On the contrary, it expands, and attacks any group or even individuals. The slanders which have been heard at various times against the Society are the result of the more general tendency of mankind to accuse, to maintain a divisiveness, to undervalue others, so that they themselves can appear better. Doesn't the same thing happen every day in our society? One family speaks contemptuously of another. Trade union organisations, political parties, professional groups attempt to annihilate one another. Even states launch themselves against one another. And, naturally, behind all this is the unconscious, which resists the new aspects, ideas which differ from those that each group embraces. Any difference, any change, and, above all, any new current brings about upheaval, causes slanders, creates opposition. Man is polarised towards what he knows and fights to hold on to it, because he fears that the unknown will bring him out of his separateness, even if the unknown is positive.

All these observations made me even more firm in my decision to develop discernment. This became a need for me, because I realised that it is only when the disciple learns to discern the depths of things that he can live without being troubled in the midst of the negative events and situations of life. And, naturally, it is only when he is not upset by these that he is able to do something to help a solution to come to the shared human problem: the separateness which brings with it condemnation and slander.

TRIALS

And then the trial came! The first great trial for all the disciples, for the Society, for the progress of the work. And this happened 22 days before the third year of my discipleship was completed. A little before I was informed of the news, the inner Master had prepared me to receive it with strength.

That morning I had accompanied my mother to the KAT Hospital because she had broken her arm. The pain of the people in the hospital had affected me and I felt weakened, with great concern for human illnesses and their endless torments. When I returned home, I began a meditation in order to recover myself, and yet again the existence of absolute Good behind every pain, every illness and misfortune was confirmed for me. A current of power then flooded me and I abandoned myself to the supreme power which possesses wisdom and manifests its love for everything.

It was in this state that an unexpected telephone call found me. A disciple, beside herself, told me that the Master and his wife had been involved in a traffic accident and were in the KAT Hospital. She didn't know what condition they were in, but it seemed to be very serious. I got ready at once and went immediately to the hospital from which I had returned a few hours before. The Master and his wife were not at all well. When I arrived at the hospital, she was already in the operating theatre, undergoing emergency surgery, because she had many injuries and was haemorrhaging, mainly in the left leg. The Master, however, was in a different room, where the doctors couldn't decide whether he should be operated on, in spite of the many fractures to his left leg and the pain that he was in.

What was causing particular concern was the previous history of the Master's health. At an early age he had suffered from Hodgkin's disease, from which at that time he had been in danger of dying. The help of the doctors and the spiritual healing which he performed on himself cured him completely, but the leg which had been injured by the accident was particularly aggravated by the previous illness. In any event, the doctors are always very cautious when there are such medical histories. For this reason, they were not able to make any forecasts in the case of the Master. They also said that they would not decide upon the operation without the written consent of his wife. And so the Master remained in pain without it being possible to do anything.

When his wife's operation was over, they were taken to two separate rooms, and it was only after a few days that we managed to find a double room so that they could be together. While his wife had begun to show some improvement, he suddenly, on the third day, began to have minor embolisms, because, as the doctors explained, some lipomata had blocked the nerves of the brain. The pain continued; the operation was not decided upon. The Master's parents, his brothers and sisters, and we disciples were very worried. Frequently, the Master would seem to be absent for hours on end and then he would say a few words to us, but we soon lost him again. This crisis lasted for three days, and little by little receded. The decision on surgery was constantly put off. After 20 days of severe pain, his wife signed the consent, because it seemed that his body could now withstand this trial.

But the problem was not rapidly solved, since the doctors decided to operate on the leg partially, because of the Hodgkin's disease, which they were afraid might bring about some complication. Thus the Master underwent two operations with a few days between them. In the meantime, the pain caused him constant suffering, and all of us suffered with him. The disciples sat with the two patients in shifts and I worked more intensively at the Society in order to take care of the jobs of those who stayed at the hospital. The Master's wife was, of course, the first to leave the hospital, whereas he remained there for many days, until the doctors said that he could go home. This was followed by a post-operative period which was very difficult for all of us. It was only slowly that the Master's health was restored, but he was left with a disability in the leg which had been operated upon. Today, seven years later, the Master still uses a walking-stick, because his left leg was left shorter than the right, while he has a permanent anchylosis in his knee.

The disciples who came to see the Master and his wife when the accident occurred and in the weeks which followed were not only those who were close to him at that period. Earlier disciples who for personal reasons had discontinued their discipleship also followed the course of the illness. Even people who knew him very slightly came to enquire after his health – particularly those who had expressed strong opposition to the teaching in the past, and had qualms of conscience over what they had done and over their attitude towards the Master. Thus the room at the hospital was always packed, and the

Master, in spite of the pain that he was in, never missed an opportunity of delivering some lessons.

For the whole time that this difficult state of affairs was going on, I remained in the state of faith and strength which I had experienced on the first day when the accident occurred. This position helped me to handle the whole situation with considerable sang-froid, especially the anxiety which every so often would come to overwhelm me. However, I never ceased to study all the causes of the accident, the development of recuperation, the attitude of the disciples – which, anyway, was something very natural. Because, as I have said, the Master's accident and the many months of recuperation were the first great trial for the disciples. In all of us, enormous questions about many issues were generated. Why had the Master suffered this blow? Why had his wife been with him? What would we do if his health didn't permit him to come to the Society? Had the accident perhaps been due to unconscious fields of the disciples? And, naturally, all of us wondered how it was possible for him to always take the opportunity of teaching us something, in spite of the pain that he was in. And so, together with the distress over all this painful episode, there were also worries about our possible unconscious culpability – and about the future of our work.

I saw that I had to stand more completely on my own two feet. I had to take on my responsibilities as a spiritual healer and as President of the Society. So I focused on two things: on meditation and on the detailed supervision of all the duties of the Society. I studied in particular the relation between the disciple and the inner Master and the work which the disciple is called upon to do under his guidance. Because my meditations at that time had passed into a more composite mental field, I shall not give a detailed account of them; I shall just give some of the findings of those meditations which have to do with the accident of the Master and his wife.

As I was working constantly for the healing of the two patients, I was increasingly uniting myself with them. Thus I began to see the inner union of the couple, the roles which each of the two played. These roles, of course, apply to every couple, but I saw them above all through the Master and his wife because I wanted to understand the reasons for the double accident. I realised that it is the man who supplies the earthing of the power and it is the woman who embraces this power, takes it into her heart, and expresses it. This function is similar to the sexual act which takes place in the physical field. The woman receives the man's sperm, makes it fruitful, and gives birth to their child. This function had been explained to us many times by the Master, but I understood it much better through the specific event of the accident. I went more deeply into the two opposite roles of the giver-man and the receiver-woman. It is only when there is a receiver that the giver can be made fruitful.

In the light of these two roles, I began to study their correspondence on other levels. I saw that the same law applies everywhere. In the more specific case of the Master and the disciples, I saw that he, again, is the giver, the one, that is, who brings to the consciousness of the disciples a pure field of consciousness, and that the disciples are his receivers. If the receivers take in the energies and powers of the soul which the Master pours out, assimilate them, and make use of them, then their own spiritual broadening takes place. If, on the other hand, they resist these powers because their personality reacts against broadening, then the energies return to the Master as opposition, as refusal, and resistance. The disciples react both consciously and unconsciously to the Master, who in essence is their consciousness itself within them. The powers which are given by the Master as strength, love, knowledge become their opposites, that is, aspects of weaknesses. These weaknesses, naturally, turn against themselves, causing various psychosomatic disturbances, but they also turn against the Master, who earths the pure field of consciousness. I knew from the experiences of three years that as the Master receives the negative currents of the disciples, he experiences them within him, until their nature changes. I had seen him enter into meditation on many occasions, in order to transform into calm the various disturbances emitted by the disciples, as I have already described in an earlier chapter.

The task of making this change is carried out within the broad field of consciousness of the Master, because the disciples have not yet acquired such a field, capable of making this transformation. But since all the energies pass through the body, the bodies of Masters are frequently affected to such a degree that they become ill for a period, or even for a whole lifetime. This depends upon the intensity of the resistances which are put up by the disciples. Masters 'carry' their problem, because the disciples are not yet in a position to do so themselves on their own, as they channel the problems of the whole of mankind.

In the last period before the accident, many resistances on the part of certain disciples had manifested themselves, and the Master had said that if a positive change didn't take place, there would be danger. The negative currents had to break out somewhere, and if the disciples did not work for the change, then they would burst out upon the Master. These words, of course, even if they caused a certain amount of perplexity, were often regarded as an exaggeration, because the disciples did not possess sufficient knowledge of energies and powers, which can work miracles if used correctly, but can also cause major disasters if used negatively through opposition.

When the accident happened, the Master's words came to the minds of the disciples and gave rise to many guilt feelings. Those in particular who had recently expressed strong resistances had many pangs of conscience about the accident. They knew that each of them had played his part, had emitted, that is, his negation towards the Master-consciousness, and that his negation had attacked the specific Master as a channel of this consciousness. His own body took upon itself all the negative forces and received the blow through the driver who had caused the collision. He, again, became the channel of the unconscious of humanity who resists broadening, union, love, and of the conscious or unconscious field of negation put forward by the disciples at that time.

As I went more deeply into all this, I also remembered the episode with the snow which had occurred at an earlier date in my case. The same thing had happened then, only my resistance had been expressed through a specific obstacle, because I refused to pass on to a specific function. But in the present instance, since there was a much more general resistance to the development of the consciousness, its recipient became the main channel of that consciousness: the Master. The more I studied this happening, the more I became aware of the responsibility of each disciple towards himself and his Master – but also towards all those who, deep down, wish to overcome their own resistances.

The meditation and mental work which I was doing explained to me completely why the Master had suffered this blow. What, however, I didn't understand was why his wife had also been injured. It seemed to me that it wasn't sufficient for me to consider that this had happened because they were a couple, because they shared everything. Their union, of course, was an explanation, but not a complete one. I had to see something deeper in order for the double accident to be explained.

I continued to work systematically in order to find the answer. I started out on the basis of the role of woman, that is, of the receiver on all levels – the physical, that of the soul, the spiritual. But as the disciples are also receivers in a field of consciousness, there is a correlation between them and the Master's wife. The disciples are the personalities who receive the power of the soul in order to become spiritual people, and woman is the symbol of the receiver of all the energies and powers given by man. Consequently, the Master's wife personifies, symbolises all his disciples. But why, I wondered, should the symbol of themselves be attacked by them? Since they were in a field of intense personality, and the negation attacked the consciousness and not the form, there was no reason for an accident to happen to the person who symbolised that personality. So where was the cause of the accident to the Master's wife?

The explanation was not given to me easily, and, naturally, I was not able to bother the Master with this matter because he was in hospital in severe pain. It was necessary for me to work for many days and to practise many meditations in order to find the answer. I started out with the knowledge that man has two opposing tendencies in himself. One is the need of the personality which refuses the broadening of the ego, and the other is the need of the soul which wants this broadening. The soul's inclination constantly challenges the personality to accept evolution, to break down its resistances. These do not relate only to certain disciples, but are expressed by everybody who wishes to retain a large ego, to remain in separateness, not to extend the soul to others.

Masters encourage broadening, the development of love and the expression of the positive current. Their task is the reinforcement of the innate inclination of the soul which exists within all of us. Disciples are those who decide to work for the expression of this inclination, but because at the beginning of their discipleship they are still very immature, they are unable to reach their goal directly. For this reason there are the endless vacillations between the two currents – that of the soul and that of the ego.

The power of the soul emits very powerful currents, in order to bring about the change and to break down the personal resistances. These currents are conscious and unconscious, as are, in any event, the currents of the personality. The goal of the soul is the good, but it often has to express itself also in an apparently negative way: for example, to bring about pain or illness, in order to call forth a quest for the cause and a greater inclination of the soul. The current of the soul attacks the disciple himself, his body and his personality, the receiver, that is, of the spiritual force. It is a known fact that disciples display certain illnesses which have to do chiefly with the broadening of the heart. The difficulties are dissolved as love develops and firm establishment in the decision on unselfish functioning comes; then the current of the soul spreads out from the energy centre of the heart, which in this way discharges and is healed. Before this substantive change takes place, problems make their appearance in the disciples. Everybody has similar problems whenever they resist the flow of the soul's energy, only there is no awareness of their resistance because there is no knowledge of the energy body and its functions.

After all the work which I did, I saw that the two opposing currents that exist in the disciple attack both his aspects. That is to say, the needs of the personality return the negative energy to the consciousness and the soul's inclination brings its own current to the limited aspect of man. This aspect is the immaturity of the disciple, the receiver who refuses to grow up. But who is the receiver of the consciousness? It is the form, the female aspect, which symbolises receptivity in relation to the man, who symbolises giving. The Master's wife is a symbol of the receiver. Through her pass all the currents of the conscious and unconscious needs of the soul of the disciples. She receives at all her levels of existence all the forces of the soul which exist in the disciples and which vibrate their bodies and their personality so that they can evolve.

Since, before the accident occurred, there was, as I have said, great resistance of personality, there was also, of course, at the same time great inclination of the soul. This vibrated the personality and passed like a solvent force into the symbol of the personality, the Master's wife. Thus, when the blow came, this manifested itself in her body, as it took upon itself all the forces of the soul of the disciples which they were not able to assimilate. The wife became the receiver of all the currents. She became, I would say, a sacrifice on the part of her soul so that the disciples, who would not yet have been mature enough to receive such a current of power – which, of course, is that of all mankind, as I have said – would not be stricken.

Entering more deeply into the causes of the accident was a great revelation for me at that time. It was the first time that I had become aware so clearly of the two opposing forces in man and the constant vibrations which they cause him. I felt great respect for those two people who had taken upon themselves the currents of the disciples – who represent the whole of humanity – in order to protect them from their own forces. As human beings, of course, the Master and his wife did not have the intention of suffering the accident, but as fields of consciousness they had accepted this role.

All this inner work, which was increasingly confirmed for me as I observed the functioning of the disciples, gave rise within me to great perplexity. I wondered whether I, and all the others, were still refusing the teaching and so were not expressing it accordingly in the work which we said we had undertaken. I found this thought painful; I couldn't stand the idea that we were responsible for the accident, even if I said that we had become channels of more general human resistance. But, as I constantly studied our attitude, I was forced to accept that we still had many gaps and that the trial which we had undergone was for us to see our gaps and to decide what we were going to do. My position, as I have said, was that I should now stand on my own two feet and pass on to greater activity. I had learnt my lesson, at least to some degree.

I decided to work on the externalisation of the decision, which was frequently intercepted by new unconscious factors, new resistances. It was the trial which proves each time whether an individual is worthy of shouldering his responsibilities. Sometimes I managed it, and sometimes I didn't. The difficulty was always caused by the remains of my own weaknesses, which increased as I came into contact with the weaknesses of others – these could be disciples or people in my environment. In any event, it wasn't important who I was influenced by, because the mistake was also within me, since I didn't approach their weaknesses with strength, as this had not yet been expressed by me as it should be.

I think that this first great trial brought about the closing of a first cycle of discipleship and the corresponding expression of a first dynamic functioning. But the cycles continued and, indeed, in the course of events it seemed that at the end of each cycle another trial came, through which the disciple had to take on greater responsibilities. The trials of discipleship in no way differ from the corresponding difficulties which every individual encounters in his life. They concern questions of health, financial and professional issues, and emotional matters. Sometimes they affect one disciple more, at other times, a whole group. Whatever is the form of the trial, it does not cease to challenge the individual to exert all his powers to overcome it.

In the years which followed, many acute problems arose in the group of disciples. And I noticed that these manifested themselves roughly every three years. This, of course, was no accident. From the point of view of numerology, three symbolises realisation: the work which must be given expression as a result of a cycle of processes and experiences. But since realisation did not occur with completeness, new trials came to broaden the consciousness and to strengthen the will of the disciples.

I shall not, for the present, deal with the new trials in detail. In any event, the analysis of the trials which followed resembles that which I have just carried out. There was always the conflict between the two opposing needs of man. Simply by way of information, I will state that the Master had another very serious illness – specifically, a urinary infection – which kept him in hospital again for many days. In addition, a group of disciples who had decided to engage in a craft industry by producing ceramic jewellery to support the Society's work went through a very difficult financial crisis, which was due to their inexperience.

Apart from these events, each one separately was put to the test every so often by a personal or family problem, to which I shall refer where there is a reason for this, so that the meanings of the teaching can be better understood.

No one endures the trials of life easily, and for that reason, whenever a new problem made its appearance in any area, the disciples would ask the Master:

"Very well, but why has another obstacle come now? What was necessary?"

"For it to have come", he would answer, "means that that's the way it should be. It wants to show you something, some new step which you must take internally, in order for you to gain strength and overcome it externally. The disciple is like an athlete who trains continuously in order to overcome the obstacles of the body and to make correct use of his powers. And it is only when he arrives at a high level that he can take part in competitions, that he can make a mark in the world, that he can demonstrate his achievements.

"This, anyway, is the essential meaning of sport: the development of the powers, which are then projected before other people, in order to teach them about the existence of these powers, which exist as potentialities within everybody. On another level, the disciple exercises his spirit, in order to express energies and powers of the soul, so that these are recognised by people and to encourage them in their own efforts.

"When, after many trials, the disciple learns to overcome the obstacles, he is ready to show others the path which he himself has covered, to become, at a certain level, of course, their Master."

"But you have urged us from the very first day to show the things we are learning while we are still ignorant. Why do you do that?"

"Because in this way boldness increases, and this leads to greater and easier performance. But this is what an experienced educator or trainer does. He encourages athletes who are beginners to demonstrate even their minor attainments to a small circle of people, who are usually all young athletes. Similarly, in the early stages of discipleship, the Master urges the disciple to express himself in the group of disciples, of his fellow-disciples, I would say. Such expression boosts his morale and prepares him for a more broadened expression, until gradually he takes on much greater responsibilities, until, that is, he spreads the teaching to many people, since that's what he is being trained in."

"So then, when at some point all the individual difficulties cease and the weaknesses are broken down, the trials should also stop. Isn't that so?"

"Yes, naturally that's the way it is. At least as regards the cycle of discipleship which involves broadening and the assimilation of the individual ego into a broader ontological field."

"But if that's the way it is, why do Masters also undergo so many trials? Since the cycle that the disciples are going through has closed for them, they shouldn't have accidents or fall ill."

"The inner Master, who always undertakes to protect the disciples, allows the negative currents to strike at the level of existence of Masters. If this didn't happen, these currents would have to express themselves on one or more disciples, thus interrupting their progress, which has not yet advanced sufficiently for them to have the power to resist the energies. As to this Master, you mustn't forget that he too continues to be a disciple on other levels. Evolution is continuous, and only the Absolute does not evolve, since it is at one and the same time all the fields of consciousness."

"Consequently, since Masters constantly undergo trials, this painful process never ends. That is depressing."

"No, it isn't. Because for Masters the pain has ended and only the process continues, and this is happiness and not pain. Because pain is due to the resistances of the ego, but when the individual ego has been assimilated to the ontological ego, then every trial is simply a continuation of progress in the fields of conscience."

"That is to say, it is only when the disciple becomes a Master like you that he ceases to be tormented by the obstacles."

"Again you personify the issue on to me. This is not the answer. The disciple ceases to suffer, to be in pain, to regard trials as painful when he unites himself with the inner Master, when he then follows all the directions of the higher consciousness without any resistance to them. Then his own discipleship begins in other fields of existence, and this is a discipleship which takes place simply, without haste, without desires, because it is revealed to him that in whatever field he finds himself, this is the same as all the others."

"And a last question, Master. Why is the work expressed in the world by the disciples, who make so many mistakes, and not by Masters, some of whom have overcome all human errors and obstacles, while others have overcome many of these, depending on their evolution?"

"But it's expressed by both. The world needs both the field of the Master and that of the disciple. In any event, how would the disciple evolve if he didn't extend himself towards humanity and if he didn't express this broadening through a specific task?"

"And so it's for this reason that you tell us to perform service, so that we ourselves will evolve?"

"Not only for that reason. Because evolution is never only individual; it is also of the group. We evolve in evolving others, but we evolve others through our own evolution."

"Yes, this has been demonstrated many times. Whenever a disciple helps someone else, he is at the same time helped himself. He learns something, he understands something, or he simply feels better. And this interaction, this bonding, the cohesion of everything is inconceivable, enchanting."

"The inconceivable is God. Union is God. Happiness is again God. With Him we are all learners, disciples and Masters alike."

And here the discussion would stop, the teaching would stop, and the questions would stop. And the path of realisation, which transforms trials into happiness, would begin. Until a new difficulty came and the same processes began again in the same way or other ways, which, however, end in the one thing, in the one entity in everyone and everything, which leads man to open his heart and to embrace the whole world.

THE MASTER IS ONE; THE DISCIPLE IS ONE

When the numbers of members of the Society had shown a considerable increase, the Master told us to visit other spiritual centres also, so that we could cross-check our experiences with them, and hear the teaching that was given there. Moreover, he advised us to invite disciples of other Masters to the Society in order for us to learn from them what they had to say to us. So we began such work, and members of other centres came to the Society, or we went to them. Whenever we heard that some Master was in Greece, we would go to meet him, to get to know him personally, to ask him questions about the religion or the philosophy which he represented.

All these contacts were, of course, of great interest, and particular when we got to know a Master. But, because at that time I had a dependence upon our own Master, I didn't seem necessary to me that I should learn something other than the teaching I was already receiving. Certainly, I liked to be with a Master, to receive the eradiation of his soul, to hear his words. But at the same time I had the tendency to say to myself that the best of all was my own Master. Thus, I found various grounds for refuting or belittling the others. I would say, for example, that I didn't like the prayers or hymns which they recited, or that the knowledge which they conveyed to us about their religion left me indifferent, or confused me, instead of helping me. I didn't always admit these thoughts, but my attitude showed that I wasn't ready to accept that anyone else was as great as our Master. Apart from two instances where the presence of the Masters was truly impressive, because, as the Master said, and it was confirmed for us, they were very great entities, in the other contacts which we made, I was left cold, or even became negative.

The Master saw my reactions and pointed out the gaps to me, showing me the unconscious which was being expressed through my specific actions. Sometimes I couldn't find anywhere to park my car, and so my contact with a Master would be delayed; sometimes I developed a headache when one was speaking, and sometimes

I would forget to ask the question which the Master had advised me to address to him. The rebukes over such events were accompanied by the analysis that I had a divisive attitude, that I was showing an attachment to one person, that I was not uniting myself with the entity, the inner Master. Naturally, I went on finding excuses, or opposing the union of soul which I didn't want to engage in.

"But, Master", I would say, "why should I listen to what they say about Buddhism or Hinduism? You teach us union with God, and that's the only thing I want."

"Have you ever heard the Master, Mrs Klairi, speak against a certain religion, or even against certain spiritual centres? All religions, all teachings lead always to the entity. What did I say to you when you were worried about whether someone of another religion can become a member of the Society? Do you remember? I told you that whatever religion he belongs to, he doesn't cease to be a human being, a part of one entity, of the one God."

"That I understand, because, in any event, I've argued that ever since I was young, but I don't understand how such knowledge will help me. The road I'm following meets my needs completely."

"No, Mrs Klairi. Here something unconscious is being concealed. You don't want to accept the entity of the other Masters because you are still attached to your own Master. But this is a mistake; it limits you. All the roads which people follow lead always to the One. Each person has a faith, a separate course, but in the end all faiths lead to God. The era of Synthesis has begun, and the inner Master brings unification; it is that which you are being taught, and not dogmatic separateness. Man, though he advances through his own religion, must at the same time accept the others, because the differences are only superficial. And the persons of the Masters are also simply persons; the consciousness within them is one, although, of course, there are many different fields of evolution in the Masters also. But beyond all these things, the one consciousness, the one Master, the supreme God lies hidden."

"I've noticed that the disciples of other Masters don't accept you easily – or at all. And yet their Masters, in speaking of you, say that you are a Master, they recognise your entity. But that doesn't make them accepting, just as I'm not accepting."

"The recognition of this Master here is not enough to dissolve the astral relation which they have with their own Master. But I repeat to you that you are serving a discipleship in the intellect, and through that you are called upon to overcome preferences for any form of person, doctrine, philosophy, etc. Our aim is union with the entity and disengagement from the form. We love the form, but we are not dependent upon it. So I would recommend that you study through books what the other religions teach. That will help you to find the one common field within all of them and to accept more easily the different forms which the Master manifests."

I knew that my problem was neither the religions nor their various formularies. What I found it difficult to do was to overcome my need to rely upon one person, and to begin to rely upon myself. It was for that reason that the Master urged me to look for the essence within everything. I had already started to meditate on the deeper meaning of 'Master', and after each meditation, I took a small step towards his inner nature. Of course, the concepts which I conceived had to do in each case with my own corresponding needs. If I felt unprotected from the unseen enemies of my weaknesses, then I would envisage the inner Master as a swordsman or knight. If I was feeling in a weakened state, I saw him playing the role of father. And whenever I felt him to be somewhat distant, he was projected for me as a hermit and ascetic. All these things, and various others, were correct, of course, but they showed only one part of the truth about his entity, that part which I needed at the time. In any event, since within each person there are such conscious or unconscious qualities of fatherhood, protection, and so on, what was projected for me didn't reveal to me anything different about the Master.

In order to help us to advance to a greater depth, the Master frequently gave us meditations in which we invoked an evolved spiritual being and passed into union with it. This being could be a saint, an adept, divinity of our trinitarian religion, or of another religion, or an unseen entity which with its spiritual power carried out some task on the planet, or in the solar system, or even in the galaxy. For a space of time we meditated with this inner union which we established with some spiritual being, and then the Master would introduce a new entity into the meditations, saying that they are all aspects of the one Master. I was often saddened when I had to leave behind – as I thought – one saint and seek help from another. I felt like an unfaithful wife who denies her husband, or a daughter who denies her father. The Master insisted, however, that these changes should take place, so that we should not become attached to one form or one manifestation only. "The Master is one", he always said to us, "just as the disciple is one."

I had heard many times that the Master is the consciousness and the disciple the unconscious, but I had great difficulty in overcoming my attachments. I was bound up with the forms of the holy entities, just as I was bound up with the form of the Master. This, in any event, also occurred with the personalities of the disciples – and of everybody. I had my preferences and repressions, which bound me to themselves. I was unable to accept that all of us disciples are one thing, in spite of the fact that I had accepted the intellectual analysis which said that what makes us one is our shared field of consciousness.

The Master, of course, guided us always to advance to deeper levels. One day he told me that the moment had now come for me to meditate on the nature of the diffuse Master and not on his qualities and his manifestations. I knew that this had to happen, and I began to prepare myself for the outcome, whatever it would be, of such meditation. I was, moreover, glad, because I knew how much this particular meditation would help me over many matters.

The first time that I carried out this meditation, I saw a circle before me. In this there were other, smaller, circles, which seemed to fill it, to be its parts. I realised that the large circle was the Master and the smaller ones were his disciples, who were within his consciousness. The totality of the range of consciousness of the disciples was the total range of the Master. I noticed that within each small circle there were other smaller ones, which, again, filled the small circle. These were, as I understood it, the human fields of consciousness which each disciple has within him. The pattern resembled totals with their subtotals, as we are taught in mathematics.

I described this meditation to the Master, who told me that it was correct, because it gives the fields and the sub-fields. He explained that human consciousness is contained within the disciple, and that his is also contained in the consciousness of the Master. He added, however, that the work was incomplete. It provided, of course, the structure for the relationship between the different fields, but it didn't show their nature, and, particularly, the nature of the Master, which he had told me to explore in depth. He told me to carry out a second meditation, in order to find the right answer, and not to avoid deepening in the truth.

I realised that the Master was right, because I hadn't been entirely satisfied by my work either; it was as if something was missing. So I began the second meditation on the same subject. This time, a sun – the source of radiance, of life, of light – appeared before me. I realised that the sun was the symbol of the Master, the nature of the giver, on which I had meditated on another occasion. On observing its rays, I saw that these are the channels of the radiance which the light brings to the planets. Consequently, the disciples must be firm in the position of these channels in order to earth the work of the Master, as the rays earth the radiance of the sun. As I advanced intellectually in the study of the solar systems, I saw that these are boundless, and so one could say that, correspondingly, Masters are boundless. Some, of course, are of a greater and others of a lesser range of consciousness, as is the case with the size of the suns throughout the universe.

Satisfied with this work, I went again to report on it to the Master. I told him that the Master is the giver, that this is his nature. That there are many Masters, just as there are many suns. I waited for his confirmation, and I thought as well that in this way I would demolish what he had told me – that there is only one Master. He was not one, he was many – this is what I had seen from the symbols of the many suns.

The reply this time was very emphatic, devastating: "No, Mrs Klairi. Again you've avoided seeing the nature of the Master. You've remained only with his manifestation, with what he gives and his giving nature. And do you know why you are doing that? To prove to me that there are many Masters and so you have every right to be a disciple of only one of them. Naturally, each disciple has his Master, just as each planet has its sun. But all the suns and all the planets are in the same universe. Similarly, all Masters with their disciples belong to one overall, boundless Master. You have failed to extend yourself beyond the forms, because, quite simply, you wish to retain your ego. Go and carry out another meditation, many meditations, until you bring me the result I've asked you for. You are to look for the nature of the Master, and not his structure and manifestations. Have you understood?"

Had I understood? Of course I had. So back to the beginning again, until I overcame the resistance. But when I settled down to meditate, I saw that my body had for a considerable time an inexplicable disturbance within it, as if I was afraid of something. Before I went on with the meditation, I had to find first of all the cause of my fear, so that I could calm down. I then remembered the words of the Master, that he does not have an ego, that he considers that he does not exist. So this is what I was afraid of, his non-existence. Because if the Master didn't have an ego, then I who was serving my discipleship with him would one day have to become like him. And this, of course, I didn't like. I wanted to have my ego, even in the limited form that it had. I remember that at least an hour passed before I dominated these ideas and took the decision to continue with the meditation.

The first thing I saw was again a sun. This time, however, I did not remain only in its radiance, but allowed myself to go into it. To understand what was hidden in its nature, what made a sun radiate continuously, what was the truth about the Master. As I entered into the sun, I realised that while there were vast energies and powers in there, nevertheless none of these remained entrapped in the sphere of the sun. All of them constantly spread out all around, so that a feeling of an absolute void, of non-existence was created. I went on to another sun, and then to another, and everywhere I saw the same feature, nothingness, the void, shining all around.

Consequently, all Masters are one thing, they are the void which creates radiation around it, constantly pouring out its energies and powers. As I advanced from one sun to another and found myself in space, I again had the same feeling of emptiness. It was as though there were no difference between space and the interior of the suns, which were enclosed within the void of space.

As I had started out with the realisation that the sun is a symbol of the Master, and since the sun is a void, then the greatest Master of all Masters is the one boundless void. Form is nothing more than a manifestation of the void, of the one Master. A manifestation which becomes the fiery radiance of the natural sun, but also the soul's radiance of the Master.

To start with, I didn't like this revelation. It is by no means easy to accept that, in the end, your sole Master is intangible, empty space – nothing, that is – which you don't see, you don't feel, you don't hear. Little by little, however, as this realisation passed within me, a calm, a deliverance from the need of the person of one individual – which undoubtedly concealed my other need for the retention of my individual ego – came. In the years which followed, I meditated very frequently on the concept of the Master, on the consciousness which is within everybody and everything. And always I saw that this one consciousness vibrates the unconscious, which is the one disciple, even if he is expressed in innumerable forms. Of course, I wasn't always ready to accept that all human beings are one field, or that all Masters are again one, in spite of the differences in their evolution. I became conscious of these things over the years and with many interruptions and obstacles.

On the day that I told the Master about the third meditation, he validated it at last. He told me that the nature of the Master is precisely that: the emptiness which exists because there are no withholdings at all. And he said that this state in its highest field is total entity. Masters express, depending upon their evolution, the entity, as they advanced in its ever broader fields.

Since I had difficulty in understanding the idea of the void, I asked the Master for further explanations. He replied:

"As we have said, the one and only Master of all things is God. But what you saw as a void and thought of as the Master is only one aspect of the truth. Because in space is all the created universe, which fills it with its splendours and radiations. Similarly, within the consciousness, which you saw to be empty, there are all the fields of the conscious and the unconscious. Within the one is completeness. This is the entity, nothing and everything."

"And each Master – what is he, then?"

"But precisely the same thing, on a very small level, of course, within the whole. The Master is free of the individual ego, but is diffused into all the egos of his disciples. Thus he remains at one and the same time full and empty."

"I don't know what happens to me when you speak in this way, Master. It is as if I were encircled by a current of power. But why?"

"Because this is the current of God. And because we are speaking of Him, his power engulfs you."

"And all this creation, the countless suns, the universes, and the inconceivable details – what are they expressing in the end?"

"What would you say, Mrs Klairi?"

"I don't know; perhaps power."

"Only that? Think now."

"I can't find anything else. You tell me."

"Love, Mrs Klairi. The boundless love of God. The magic, the indescribable beauty of the universe, the harmony in nature are the offspring of love. Of the Wisdom and the Love of God."

With these words, the Master seemed to lose himself, to no longer be next to me, not to be aware of my presence. It was as if he had been emptied of everything and didn't need any communication with the world. But in this strange state, I saw something in him which I had not yet experienced. I discerned a bliss which it was impossible for me to describe or to understand with my mind. And when he returned from his journey, I would ask him:

"What have you been doing, Master, where were you, what were you experiencing?"

"I wasn't doing anything, I wasn't anything, it was God, it is always God."

"You have become another person, as if you didn't have reason, or thoughts, or feelings. Is that how it was?"

"What am I to say? One way or the other, I don't know. He who is everything knows."

"When will we disciples pass into this state?"

"That is a matter for the Most High, who knows what must happen with everybody and everything. For the present, work with regularity. Meditate, unite yourself with the super-ego, and perform service. Everything else will come of its own accord. Let's recite a ritual now, to hymn Him."

And he would begin to sing in his superb voice, which always thrilled all the disciples. Those of us who were with him would sometimes join in the ritual with him and sometimes enjoy the melody and experience the vibrations of the rituals. The Master would change form again; he would take on an expression of magic, as if he had been carried away by the partaking of the music, as though a divine gentleness had flooded him.

And we looked on and wondered. And those who had had doubts as to the entity of the Master changed their attitude towards him. Because they saw that 'something else' which exists, which can't be explained, which can't be described, but whose nature overwhelms man, breaking down the bonds of the mind and of the emotions. And we all wanted to be like him, to become what he is.

That was until one day when I too experienced this gift for a few minutes. The Master was performing a ritual and I was seated, as always, next to him, in the first place on the right. All around were the other disciples. I was looking at him and enjoying the melody when suddenly his body disappeared from before me and in its place remained bright sparks which rolled up and down like a pillar of light in the place of its bearer. And as I looked at this incredible change, little by little the brightness disappeared too, and in its place there was just an empty space, a total void... It was as if this took me into itself, made me like it, an existence whose texture and essence I had never imagined. I was and I was not; I existed through another dimension of absolute completeness.

The ritual ended, the Master appeared before my eyes again in his familiar form, and I came to earth in the usual place. This was a small taste, a small transition which came to show me another state of consciousness, in which everything was simple, very simple, where there was no thought, or need. As though the one Master had wished to show me, the disciple, his boundless existence. Similar revelations happen sometimes to the disciples, when they need them, for them to establish themselves in a position. No single one is exactly like the others, because the needs of the disciples themselves show constant changes.

What was confirmed for me through that few minutes of experience which I had was the boundlessness and completeness of the higher self. It was a prompting to accept the one Master who passes into the consciousness of the one disciple, in whatever way he needs him. And I simply thanked the higher self for the sweet taste which it granted me that day.

In the years which followed, I experienced other moments of ecstasy and magic. But the Master didn't leave me in these for long, but he urged me always to have my mind and my thoughts turned towards the work and spirituality. To begin with, his attitude upset me, because I would very much have liked to be continuously in ecstasy. But the disciple, every disciple, must be a channel of spirituality. He is not taught only for himself, because then not even he would become a spiritual human being. Spirituality means love, action, service, and not personal satisfaction.

I remember that at one time a strange phenomenon used to happen to me regularly. I would look in the mirror and little by little the shape of my face would become dim, more and more dim, until in the end it disappeared completely. However much I looked, I couldn't see its reflection. After a few minutes my face would begin to take shape again, only its form appeared clearly before me. The first time this happened to me, I was astonished, I didn't know what it was, and I thought it was marvellous and incredible.

I began to repeat the experiment, and it always produced the same result: I lost my face. This happened especially easily when I was in the peaceful environment of our house in the country. I had the feeling then that as I had no immediate obligations, thoughts left me and my mind passed into a dimension of emptiness. When I looked in the mirror, to begin with I saw myself with my eyes, but later it was as if I was looking at myself from the empty dimension of the mind, with some other vision which doesn't look at the natural field. It looked only at its own field, its emptiness, and so I didn't see anything in the mirror.

The phenomenon of the disappearance of the form was fascinating, as was that of the recovery of its image in the mirror. I experimented, I played, I wondered what was happening – in general, I was much concerned with all this that was going on. In the end, I reported it to the Master, who spoke just a single sentence: "Don't take any notice of these things, Mrs Klairi". And then he began to talk about something else, very practical and specific. I was disappointed, of course, with his reply, but I also came to earth in the reality of life with its great needs. I know very well that the Master didn't leave me in that state because I was not yet ready. I couldn't put together the two aspects, the emptiness with the fullness, and so I was in danger of being led astray by the magic and the calm of the one, while ignoring the other. If that had happened, I would never have arrived at the goal, which is union with the Absolute, with God.

Since all the experiences which I have described may seem strange and unbelievable, I shall make an analysis before ending the chapter. Nothing is strange, all things exist, everything is very natural. It is just that man does not know them because his unconscious is large; it is the disciple who is trained to learn. But the consciousness, the one Master, knows all of them, the visible and the invisible, the existent and the non-existent. For that reason there is no mystery, everything can be explained, everything is very simple.

Emptiness, in which all forms disappear, is a part of the consciousness of each individual, and not only of the Masters. The difference is that the Masters know this, whereas people do not have such knowledge. They know only their form, and some also know the energies within it. But the void is still unrealised, and so it takes them by surprise whenever it is revealed. We all have the same nature deep down, we are empty and filled simultaneously. In our body, innumerable explosions of energies and forces take place, and these have the purpose of rendering us empty one day, of assimilating us to the solar nature of the Masters. Each little experience leads us to an understanding of this nature, until one day we are able to be at one and the same time empty and filled. But for such a transition to take place, a cycle of action in the natural field has to be completed, and for that reason the Master urges us also to accept all forms and work for them. If this work has not gone first, no transition of consciousness is completed, there is always an unsupplied item which leads the disciple astray because of his premature tendency towards deliverance.

What happened to me that day when I saw the Master become first energy and then a void was a gift from the supreme Self, as I have said. It was as if the Master-consciousness was talking to the disciple-unconscious and saying: “Look at what man is. He is the form, the soul, and the spirit. He is the triune entity. You must become that. Because that is the will of the Self for all beings.” And I became that for a few minutes. I tasted the magic of union, of diffusion, and of fullness. And then the inner Master earthed me again in the form, to work for it, as He does for the whole universe.

Master and disciple, the conscious and the unconscious. In us and all around us are these two aspects of the Entity. We begin first to recognise that some people are disciples and others are Masters. Then we advance to the broader realisation and we see that the Master is one and the disciple is one. And when this concept also has completed its cycle, then we arrive at the next stage. We connect the Master with the disciple, we see them as a single whole, like knowledge and ignorance cancelling each other out, and the One, God, the Supreme Self of all things is structured.

EPILOGUE

The book is finished! I'm holding the manuscripts in my hands and leafing through them before I send them to the printer's. I can't believe it. For four years I've torn up, written, then torn up again, and the book 'The Master' looked as though it was never going to be finished. And then, suddenly, it took off, as if on its own accord, and was ready before my eyes. Twenty-two whole chapters! How is that possible?

Thoughts begin to overwhelm me. Should I perhaps tear it up again and start again in a new way? Am I perhaps not giving the reader what I wanted to give him? Why was there such ease in the writing after four years of difficul-

ties? I have to find the answer to all these questions before I begin the publication process. And I remember the words of the Master which he said to us often: "Look deep inside your mind, the answer is there, the truth is there. Look to find it."

And I begin to search with the help of ten years' knowledge and experiences. I search out the cause of this brief piece of work of authorship, which has puzzled me so much. And while I think and the answer doesn't come, I suddenly remember the numbers and decide to study them to see what they symbolise. I've received so much instruction from numerology. So I will use it on this matter, as I have done over many things up to now. And I begin the study.

Four years, 22 chapters, 25 days of writing work, ten years of discipleship. I must, then, work with these four numbers, the four symbols which are given to me, in order to understand and find the answers that I want.

I begin with the first number: four. This is the symbol of matter, of form, of the body. It is the base on which the whole spiritual edifice rests. Without the body, man would not acquire consciousness, his mind would not develop. It is in the body, in the brain, in the heart that ideas are brought to birth, are rendered fruitful, and then find expression. So for four years the meaning of the book was within me, was being worked upon in the mind, was grow-

ing, was developing, and suddenly was born quickly, as a child is born from its mother's womb.

This answer begins to satisfy me, but, again, I find the period of preparation long. I had written the previous books in three to four months each, without this being preceded by so many difficulties. Why was this? Little by little the ideas become clearer in my mind. My previous subjects had been better known when I began my discipleship, and with the help of the teaching I was able to set them in order more easily. But the subject of the Master was completely unknown to me, and before acquiring the necessary knowledge of it, it wasn't possible for me to give expression to it. A long period of time was needed for it to be brought to birth in my mind, and then be born on paper.

I now go on to the second number, the 22 chapters of the book. But what does 22 symbolise? The closing of a circle, numerology says. But what circle? What closed with what I have written? This is considered to be only a very little information from the teaching I have received. What can the reader understand from the 22 chapters about so great a subject? I look at the title of the first chapter: "Who is the Master?" A sentence containing a question. And this is followed by the procedures, the individual answers, the aspects of the Master, to reach its culmination with the last title: "The Master is One; The Disciple is One". Perhaps the reader will think that I chose the titles, and that it's not in any way strange that I should have found the appropriate beginning and a correct ending for the book. And yet it didn't happen like that. I didn't think them up at all. All the titles sprang from my mind entirely spontaneously, incredible as that may seem. Nor is the book as if I'd written it; it's as though it wrote itself on its own, because, quite simply, the time had come for it to be written. In any event, I now know very well that no work is human. All are works of the entity and are expressed through man, depending upon his will in each case.

In order to understand what circle closed with this book, I begin the study of the next number, so I can be helped by studying what the number symbolises. This is 25 – the number of days that were needed for the 22 chapters to be written. Although numerology extends to all the numbers, the better known are one to 22. For that reason, I add together the two digits, two and five, which, of course, give me seven. Seven is synthesis, a synthesis of certain factors which structure a whole. I read again all the titles of the chapters and I see that in fact these make up a composite presentation of the concepts of the teaching.

Naturally, as I have said, this is only a first presentation, but it is global. Consequently, the first circle was completed with the synthesis of the initial concepts of the composite teaching which I received at the beginning of my discipleship.

And now there remains only the last number, the ten years of this discipleship. Ten symbolises the wheel. I remember immediately that the first dream which I described to the Master was that in which I saw that I had to become the centre of the wheel and move it by power and will. In studying the symbol of the wheel in relation to the content of the book, I see that in this the position of the centre has been expressed, but also that of the circumference. A central point of a stable position is occupied by the Master, and on the circumference are the disciples, who express the swings, the difficulties, and the problems. It also seems that it is the Master who pulls the strings, gives the guidelines, and teaches balance to the disciples.

With the analysis of the number ten, the study of the numbers is completed. It can be summed up in this way: the book on the Master was being brought to birth in my mind for four years, and was expressed on the completion of a ten-year cycle of discipleship, in which two opposing aspects are apparent: the ontological, dynamic, and stable position and the various weak manifestations of man. The chief characteristic of the book is the great battle of the personality with the inner consciousness, the entity of man. Apart from this conflict, certain initial stages of awareness, as experienced by myself and the other disciples at that time, are given.

We are speaking of cycles of experiences, cycles of discipleships and awareness. This first book is the first cycle, the basis for those which follow. The concept of the Master is a vast one; it covers all concepts, it concerns all things, from the smallest to the greatest. Also vast is the concept of the disciple, since this includes the unconscious, which I would say is bottomless. Disciple and Master are two opposite fields which little by little, over the years and with very intensive and systematic work, begin to unite, to become a single whole. What links the conscious with the unconscious are the energies and powers of the soul, which vibrate the personality, so that it can express the deeper self.

By these thoughts I see that my questions have been answered. The book gives what I wanted it to give, the great oppositions which all of us conceal within us, and the causes of the reactions to the teaching. It also gives some initial information on the deliverance which comes when man begins to express his self. Perhaps some readers expected something else from the book on the Master, some more profound concepts, or a more theoretical analysis. But I believe, as I have already said, that all these things only take on true meaning and become knowledge when they are checked against action and experience in everyday life. In the books which will follow, more and more data and more composite analyses on the inner man and the entity will gradually be given.

The second book, which also has 'The Master' as its main title, will deal more with the world of man's soul.

This, of course, does not mean that it will not speak of the problems of the personality. On the contrary, these may be even more intense, because the work of the soul calls forth strong oppositions. But the oppositions find other means of settlement when the soul has begun consciously to surface. And the teaching is different when the inner Master is recognised and becomes the magnetic pole of the soul's energies and powers. Thus the content of the second book will speak of the conscious effort of the soul to be united with the Entity. An effort which requires time, patience, and stability, until the result is achieved and the ontological self is manifested through the personality.

Before I complete the first book, I would like to address a big 'thank you' to the Master, who has supported me for these ten years and always supports me whenever I need his advice. I am speaking personally, but also collectively, on behalf of all his disciples who are still with him, and of those who, for various reasons of their own, have broken off their discipleship. I hope that all alike will make use daily of the knowledge which they have received, in order to be delivered from their human weaknesses. Because the Master is within us, and this has to be realised by all mankind. It is him we are taught to follow, to obey, until we come to express him. The Master in the natural field refers always to the inner Master, teaching us how to recognise him in everyone and in all things, and above all in our own selves.

I would also like to thank the Master's wife, who in her own way supports his work. Because I know she has all the disciples in her heart and suffers with all of them over all their problems.

I hope the disciples will vindicate her sacrifice, and that of the Master, by spreading more and more the work of spirituality to as many people as possible.

REVIEWS

I have received and read avidly your book "The Master". Your thoughts, your reflections, you endeavours, your aims, your hopes have truly impressed me. In such a way that all the things which you describe your Society as doing teaches maturity, truth, the way of acquiring self-knowledge, which, unfortunately, is so lacking in present-day man! Our country has it in it to produce 'Socrateses', and your Master, from what you describe, brought him before me at full length with all his virtues. I was moved by your valour and your wholehearted dedication to the Society... Accept my admiration for your poet Master.

Yannis Kofinis – Writer

Your admiration for the Master is expressed in a manner which is unfeigned; it becomes Love through his Person for something more universal, which embraces Virtue and Wisdom, Beauty and Knowledge, with the most profound approaches to the Supreme Truth. I consider that it is this Truth that you serve, as you write about the Master.

I read your work, the fruit of experiences and inner ferment, with interest. It is replete with essence of life. Your mind sees deeply into things, it reviews, it professes. Not simply to establish Ideas, to argue them - this is of little importance. But in order to win on their 'road' to Action the inner victory, confirming the value of Morality and Duty towards our hidden self.

Tasos Anagnostou - Writer

Life is a great teacher, and to become aware of the universal powers of the 'self', a great deal of initiation and meditation is required. You have passed through a number of fields of spiritual ascent with the help of the Master; and one can only admire the formulation of your thoughts in a book which has as its centre the spiritual power of man, his entity and personality, and, above all, his divine origin.

The wise gradation of the chapters and the revelation of the power of meditation is impressive. And the arguing of the universal 'partaking' of man in his multifaceted entity by the means of meditation establishes this spiritual piece of writing as a worthy work of life and discourse.

Nikos Kavroulakis - Writer

In 'The Master', among other things, I discovered dynamic truths, conclusive meditations on love, the need for balance of soul, endless spiritual improvement, and, generally, a correct and noble order in human relations.

Rare works like 'The Master' grant me moments of moral and spiritual re-ordering, so that the mind is detached from possible pointless and harmful actions in the behaviours of individuals in general.

Yannis Tserionis – Writer

Klairi Lykiardopoulou, in her book "The Master" has recounted her experiences arising out of knowing the Master of the Society of Servers and what she was taught by him. She speaks of the knowledge and consciousness which lead man to greater self-knowledge and autonomy. The writer, starting out from her experiences with a specific Master, broadens the concept of the 'Master' by pointing out that we are all taught every day by everything. And thus she presents to us, in a lucid way, with a profound knowledge of her topics, and an awareness of her responsibility towards present-day man, Life the Master, people the Master, our self the Master. Thus, 'The Master' is a book about self-knowledge, and the benefits to us from a reading of it are very great.

On-Going History of Modern Greek Literature (VOL. 9)
Michalis Staphylas – Writer

Your work is truly important, a substantive labour, an outstanding contribution to our prose-writing, because your discourse is true, since it faces problems, broadens the spiritual horizons, and becomes diachronic, a source of life, action, and reaction, proposition and denial, faith and confession. Your narrative and the presentation of your issues are impressive.

This work of yours – dedicated to the Master Kakalidis – does you particular honour and sets the seal on your sensitive inner world, Man, who knows how to exist and to journey in light with the heart outside hate and the mind alert to the good. The MASTER is a testimony which is moving, which drives away darkness, which teaches.

Mitsos Katsinis – Writer

Klairi Lykiardopoulou

Klairi Lykiardopoulou was born in Athens. She went to school at the American College and completed her studies in pedagogy in the United States. She has traveled around the world and has met many different cultures.

Her life changed radically after her acquaintance with Master Dimitris Kakalidis, founder of the "Servers' Society" Spiritual Centre, in 1980. With his guidance, she received his teaching on self-study, on the emergence of the spiritual nature of man and on practicing Spiritual Healing as a way of life. For almost three decades now, she is President of the Society.

She contributed to the structuring of the Servers' Society Healing Section, for which she constantly works by training new healers. Answering unselfishly to the need of the fellow-man, she has met thousands of people who sought help for health, personal, or family problems. On a daily basis she accepts patients who ask for her help through Spiritual Healing, and continues to receive letters of thanks from patients who were healed, either through contact healing or distant healing. Extracts of her book "Spiritual Healing", first published in 1987 in Greece, were presented in sequels in a newspaper of wide circulation, in 1989.

For her literary work she receives commending reviews and is widely appreciated by the country's intellectual world. Extracts of her books have been included in anthologies and literary magazines. Her trilogy about the role of man, woman and the couple was approved by the Hellenic Ministry of Education and Religious Affairs for school libraries. In interviews at the state channel and the radio she has emphasized the need for all people to know and express their true nature.

She has already written 19 books, conveying her personal experiences of her discipleship and developing issues concerning various aspects of life with examples of everyday life, always based on the teaching she has received. An overall presentation of her literary work up until now was held in March 2009, where renowned writers spoke of her offer to the intellect.

Ms Lykiardopoulou continues to work for the task of the Servers' Society, which is the development of human conscience and the dissemination of spirituality.

www.ingramcontent.com/pod-product-compliance
Lightning Source LLC
Chambersburg PA
CBHW071356150726
48000CB00001B/51

* 9 7 8 9 6 0 7 3 5 0 2 7 5 *